# SOME LETTERS FROM ABROAD

## OF

# JAMES ELROY FLECKER

J. E. F., BY LAWRENCE, ON THE BALCONY AT AREYA.

[*Frontispiece.*

# SOME LETTERS FROM ABROAD

OF

## JAMES ELROY FLECKER

WITH A FEW REMINISCENCES

BY

HELLÉ FLECKER

And an Introduction by J. C. Squire

LONDON
WILLIAM HEINEMANN, LTD.
1930

Printed in Great Britain by
The Whitefriars Press, Ltd., London and Tonbridge

# INTRODUCTION

To preface this volume with a biographical summary would be to duplicate work already done in the introduction to *Flecker's Collected Poems*, published by Martin Secker. The information given there is itself greatly amplified by the letters here published. It should suffice here to give but the barest skeleton of Flecker's short life.

James* Elroy Flecker was born at Lewisham on November 5th, 1884, the eldest of the four children of the Rev. W. H. Flecker, D.D., late Headmaster of Dean Close School, Cheltenham. He went to school first at Dean Close and then at Uppingham. From 1902 to 1907 he was at Trinity College, Oxford. He then spent a year in London, partly as a schoolmaster—the practical interest in education never left him—and then went to Caius College, Cambridge, for two years, where he learnt Oriental languages with a view to entering the Consular Service. In June 1910 he was sent to Constantinople, but at the end of the summer had to return to England, and go into a sanatorium. He appeared to be cured when he returned to Constantinople in March 1911 ; was transferred to Smyrna in the following month ; and in May, at Athens, married Miss Hellé Skiadaressi. His subsequent movements, first in the East, then, as an invalid, in Switzerland, may easily be followed in the letters here printed. He died on January 3rd, 1915, at Davos, and is buried at Cheltenham. His principal works are to be found in the following volumes : *Collected Poems* (Secker), *Collected Prose* (Heinemann), *The King of Alsander* (a novel,

* He was christened Herman and changed his name.

Allen and Unwin), and the two posthumously-printed plays, *Hassan* and *Don Juan*, both published by Heinemann. He had little fame in his lifetime, though his genius was known to most of his brother poets. Nor did he live to see the production of any of the dramatic work which was the chief preoccupation of his later years. It was not until years after the War ended that Mr. Basil Dean's impressive production of *Hassan* was at last seen at His Majesty's Theatre; it is probable that even this play, which contains, perhaps, the finest pages he ever wrote, and is certainly his most ambitious production, would have been further and drastically revised had Flecker lived longer.

Any editor of Flecker's work would be well-advised in emphasising the fact of his early death. It is especially important because of the comparative lateness of his development. Mr. Frank Savery has said that when Flecker went up to Oxford " he was extraordinarily undeveloped, even for an English Public School boy." He did not stand forth in his full splendour as a poet until the end; and, although there are no very early letters in this volume, I do not think it is fanciful to notice a gradual deepening of judgment even in the correspondence of his last five years. No young man is on his oath in letters to other young men. There is a danger of our forgetting this; just as, to take a very extreme case, people who express amazement at some of the more absurd actions of Shelley tend to overlook the fact that most of them date from years so early that the poppy of oblivion might have been scattered over them had the poet survived until seventy, and that, extravagant as Shelley was at thirty, he was nothing like as extravagant as he had been at twenty. I make this, I hope not superfluous, point because there are, in some of the earlier letters statements which Flecker would have modified later on, and which probably he would, even at the moment of writing, have put in a more qualified form had he been asked to express himself precisely and for publication. It would be a pity if the hasty pæans and thumpings of his private letters were to be taken as the soberest and most considered judgments of which he was capable. It must be admitted that he was always, in speech and as a correspondent, enthusiastic and combative, given to writing, on the slightest provocation, postcards packed full of championship or protest. But he had a shrewd eye for other people's overstatements, and his published critical work is judicious, illuminating, and entirely his own.

Another thing which needs to be made clear is that the letters here printed are merely the chance remainder out of many hundreds written by one who was a particularly fecund correspondent. Few young men hoard each other's letters, and most of Flecker's have disappeared. One friend with whom he corresponded most voluminously does not possess a single note from Flecker. He must have written freely to Rupert Brooke, and the correspondence between these two would have been of special interest; but what wastepaper baskets in Cambridge, railway-carriage windows in Canada, lazy blue waves in Samoa and Fiji saw the passage from human eye of Flecker's letters to his brother poet? For myself, my personal acquaintance with Flecker was of the slightest. Visiting Cambridge when he was up there, I casually met him once or twice in undergraduates' rooms at Trinity; and never got into correspondence with him until 1913, when I was shown the manuscript of *The Old Ships* and expressed unreserved admiration of it. Yet during that last year I had a good many letters from him which I did not keep, and those which survived only survived by chance.

These letters should, therefore, be treasured as fortuitous specimens of Flecker's correspondence rather than as selections from the whole body of it. They are sufficient to bring the living ardent spirit before us, the young wandering poet with his shifting moods and kaleidoscopic emotions, a being passionately serious and flippantly humorous, a laughing lover, essentially religious yet delighting in mockery, confident in his powers but not immodest about his performances, a great hater of humbug and cant, but no cynic or extremist, an affectionate friend and a generous admirer of other men's works, prejudiced to some extent on behalf of the neglected good but never vulgarly prejudiced against the popular good. He enjoyed both praising and cursing, but praising far more. And if he comes to life in these few letters he comes to life equally in the narrative into which Mrs. Flecker has interwoven them. I must leave it to others to express the admiration that must be aroused by the charm and skill of her picture of those few years of marriage ; but I may at least be forgiven if I remark that she has contrived to unite evident candour with qualities of dignity and good taste which, at the moment, we do not commonly associate with candour.

J. C. SQUIRE.

# FOREWORD

J. E. FLECKER's correspondence with friends in
England during the last five years of his life abroad—
the period of his maturer work—was chiefly concerned
with the material side of his art and life. Thus most of
his letters to Mr. E. Marsh and to Mr. John Mavrogordato contain appeals for help with reluctant editors
or theatrical managers, and might lack interest for the
reader if here and there a personal opinion or the record
of a mood did not make them valuable in the case of a
poet as impersonal as the author of the *Golden Journey
to Samarkand*.

The letters to friends residing out of England are of
more general literary interest. Mr. Frank Savery is
perhaps the only one of his correspondents abroad to
have preserved the whole or nearly the whole of the
letters received between 1910 and 1914, in spite of the
vicissitudes traversed at the outbreak of hostilities in
Germany. Most of the poet's other friends, as Mr.
R. W. Bullard or Colonel Lawrence, had such stirring
activities thrust upon them during wartime in the Near
East that it is not surprising none of their papers survived. Others did not themselves survive, including
Rupert Brooke and a very old Oxford friend, Mr.
Leonard Cheesman, who was killed at the Dardanelles.

Although the letters to Mr. Frank Savery have already
been published some time ago in a limited edition, we
believe they are, together with some of those preserved
by Mr. Marsh, Mr. Squire, Mr. Mavrogordato and Mr.
Monro, interesting enough, as revealing much of the
poet's nature in their frankness and concise style, to be
presented to the greater public.

I have at the same time endeavoured to relate some of the incidents and events I can recall from the day I first met J. E. Flecker on a Mediterranean steamer to the time when, compelled by cruel circumstances, we left Syria for Switzerland. These few reminiscences may bring before the reader something of the scenery and of the people that passed before the screen of the poet's mind at the time he was writing the poems of the *Golden Journey to Samarkand* and *Hassan,* but they do not pretend to be a biographical sketch. Of the last twenty months of his life I could say very little that would not be painful to me and also to the reader. I give an account of the poet's last moments, so that all who love him may know that the man who had written " A Coward's Song " after suffering long and bravely greeted with serenity Death the Deliverer.

My sincere thanks are due for permissions to publish these letters to Mr. J. C. Squire, to Mr. F. Savery, to Mr. E. Marsh, to Mr. Monro, and to Mr. John Mavrogordato ; also to Mr. Bullard for the interesting fragment of his letter. The photos illustrating this volume were taken (unless otherwise stated) by J. E. Flecker himself.

**HELLÉ FLECKER.**

# CONTENTS

# CONTENTS

# ILLUSTRATIONS

# SOME LETTERS FROM ABROAD OF J. E. FLECKER

## REMINISCENCES 1910

O heart that neither beats nor heaves
In that one darkness lying still,
What now to thee my love's great will
Or the fine web the sunshine weaves.

D. G. ROSSETTI.

ON June 11th, 1910, I took passage at Marseilles on board the *Crimée*, a "Messageries" cargo boat bound for Pireus, Constantinople and the Black Sea. I was going for a visit to Athens, my native town, which I had left some years before to live with my mother in Paris. I remember the sea had been rough in the Gulf of Lyons, and that I only emerged from my cabin early on the third day when the boat had reached the Messina Straits and calmer waters. I found myself looking at the ruins of Messina (the earthquake that destroyed the beautiful old city had taken place not many months before) and exchanging unimportant remarks with my neighbour. I noticed a fine black crop of hair blown back by the wind, a clear gaze, and a remarkable Norfolk jacket of greenish homespun. My first impression was that I was talking to an Irishman; he looked so much darker and more intellectually expressive than any Englishman I had ever met abroad (I had at the time never been to England, and my acquaintance with English people was based on a few diplomats and naval

officers with whom I had danced or picnicked at Athens).
It chanced I mentioned D. G. Rossetti, who was at the
time my favourite poet, and Hérédia ; this immediately
seemed to break the ice. The Straits were passed when
my neighbour said with a humorous smile, "Now I
must go below and make myself beautiful." He was
soon back, a little less dark in complexion, and we
looked on together at the fantastic outline of the Cala-
brian coast. The sea kept fairly calm that day across the
Adriatic ; in the evening there was a young moon in a
green sky, and the wake of the ship became at night a
river of silver in which sirens played.

Next morning we were in the Ionian Sea and on
coming up on deck I found the young Englishman
waiting to show me his latest poem, beautifully written
out on a large sheet of paper. It was " Pillage," and I
remember saying after I had read it : " But this is extraordinarily good for an amateur ! " and his answering
with one of his sardonic smiles : " Well, I'm not quite
an amateur you know."

In the afternoon we passed Cythera, and about mid-
night, having doubled Cape Maléa, we turned sharply
north and were caught in a breeze fragrant with thyme
and orange blossom. Flecker seemed intoxicated with
the beauty of the sea and the sky ablaze with stars.
Venus shone to the south, so sparkling and large that
it hung like a gem of liquid fire from the sky and threw
a long silver trail in the waters. We saw the sunrise—
not the gradual emerging of a reddish ball from the
morning mists, as in these northern climes, but the
God of Light leaping up from the East in full glory
and immediately ruling the world—before returning to
our cabins. A few hours later we entered Pireus Harbour, and had that strange view of Athens and the
Acropolis from the sea, looking so far away yet so clear-
cut an image high up in the air.

Our party, composed of a Scotch lady, three or four

1910: ATHENS AND THE LYCABETTUS.

1910: ATHENS AND THE ACROPOLIS.

*[To face p. 2.*

Englishmen and myself, drove up to Athens in two of those old fashioned " landaus," which were then the usual Athenian carriage. The day was a hot one, and the visit to the Acropolis before lunch was very fatiguing. Flecker seemed absorbed and hardly looked at the landscape and monuments. Later I often had the occasion of noticing he had a way of sharply taking in a view or object, never gazing long at it, but immediately either commenting on it in speech or shutting up in his mind the impression received and gazing long not at the object itself, but at that inner image with an absorbed and absent expression. That day, in spite of fatigue, his face wore a smile of intense pleasure. His first view of a land he had so often imagined was not a disappointment.

At lunch he was very brilliant and in high spirits, and immediately after, in spite of the Greek saying that " at two o'clock in summer only mad foreigners and dogs walk the streets," which was told him, he insisted on going round the town, and we wandered along the dazzling white marble pavements, half-blinded by the reverberation and the heat, to the esplanade of the Zappeion from which the view over the Acropolis and far sea is so magnificent. Then he took the train to Pireus to join his boat and proceed to Constantinople.

His impression of Byzantium on arriving there was a wonderful one. " It is difficult not to be lyrical in this divine country," he wrote, but when the first enthusiasm had cooled down he missed more and more the intellectual atmosphere of Oxford and Cambridge. " I am lonely—there is no one here I am really fond of. . . . Society here is worse than that of a small cathedral town in England. . . ." Mr. R. W. Bullard's intelligent comprehension and growing sympathy were then a great comfort to him, and he soon felt he had found a true friend. Mr. Bullard recollects on their acquaintance the following incident :

" We both liked humour in the English sense, and

strong rollicking fun with a touch of the grotesque. Indeed, it was an absurd and grotesque remark of mine which I think made him look at me with a kindly eye. It was at Candilli. We were sitting on a wall somewhere, and à propos of the local people (I think) he speculated as to what they could do for amusement. 'Oh,' I said idly, ' play with the bugs in the cool of the evening.' It is feeble enough written down, but it had just that touch of ludicrous vulgarity which appealed to him, and I so well remember how he grinned and looked at me with interest."

Concerning the work he was now set to he wrote to me : "Accounts you say, for a poet ! And why not. Fascinating tidy rows of figures all marvellously balancing and not balancing in the end and the payment of good red gold. Fortunately, half the time I can dream or read Turkish or write, as I write now to you. . . ." But in reality the work and the midsummer heat which had now set in and to which he was not accustomed tired him. I was myself, by a strange coincidence, invited to stay with friends on the Bosphorus in August, and when I saw him there by the end of that month he looked thinner, and was suffering from continual sore throat, but his spirits were high nevertheless. He then had rooms in a delightful wooden house, which he shared with other consular officials, at Candilli, one of the most picturesque villages on the Asiatic coast of the Bosphorus. There were many printed hangings on the walls, and a familiar green dragon of Dardanelles earthenware guarded the window-sill of his sitting-room.

Early in September I had returned to Athens, where I received a gloomy note telling me he was homesick and miserable owing to a cold, for which I had advised him on last seeing him to consult a doctor. He seemed thoroughly weary of the "purple East." Then shortly after came the news that he was in hospital with a bad chill which proved serious enough to necessitate his

4

STAMBOUL: A MOSQUE BY THE WALLS.

STAMBOUL: THE WALLS.

*[To face p. 4.*

being sent home to England. He was shipped on a French steamer which went direct from Constantinople to Marseilles, not stopping at Pireus on the way, as he first had thought. He watched from far the coast of Greece, which three months before he had greeted with such a glad spirit. It must have been a depressing journey for him, ill and alone with not a soul on board to speak to; yet he wrote a cheerful letter from Marseilles, quoting Theocritus and relating the incidents of the voyage.

"The passengers (the first class passengers number two) such as they are, are all quite impossible people except a conjurer, who is nice and serious. The sea has been *NHNEMOΣ* and the boat has not given a pitch since we left Constantinople. I have been reading Theocritus (as you may judge) and some English novels comfortable in my deck-chair in the sun, and only miserable that you and I can't go and live at Stromboli under the volcano—there is a glorious little village there and it is the noblest of islands.

"As we were doubling Cape Spartivento (just before you come to the Straits of Messina) a cargo-boat ran into us under my nose. It was drifting along full steam ahead without a soul on the bridge and cut right into us. If our good Commandant hadn't manœuvred—I should be writing this letter—if at all—from some nice place on the South Italian coast. We have got a large dint in our sides. I am attesting in a written document that it was all the other party's fault. Which other party, indeed, made off without so much as whistling its sorrow, on the way to Trieste."

He went straight on to Cheltenham spending on the way through Paris an evening and night in the Latin quarter, as he later confessed to me, which means he felt fairly strong after the sea journey. His family had found a sanatorium near Stroud to which he proceeded immediately.

He at first found life there very dull, but soon he made the acquaintance of a beautiful young girl who was staying there with her invalid sister and he recovered his spirits. In a letter dated October 15th, he wrote to me : " I am living high up over the plain in a forest among hills, among autumn leaves and colours very lovely. I am writing new and splendid works. . . ."

He was then working at the long poem " Don Juan from the Shadows." By the end of October the lady " lovelier than Helen of Troy " had left with her sister and he felt depressed. About this time I received that sad little poem then inscribed as " Song," and later entitled " In Memoriam," beginning—"I never shall forget that night . . ."—the haunting reminiscence of his meeting in London with a young girl he had, I believe, known at Oxford who had been slowly dying of his own complaint. In that same letter he asked for some Greek folk-songs. I sent him a small collection of these with a rough translation, and soon received " Zacho," a charming though not very close rendering of the original Greek. In November he was still working hard at " Don Juan from the Shadows." Rain had set in, and he now dreamt of going south, perhaps to Sicily, and wrote asking me if I could go there too by any chance. In December he started *Don Juan*, the play which was to keep him busy for the next three months ; and, after spending Christmas at his home at Cheltenham, he decided to leave for Switzerland, stopping a day or two in Paris on the way.

*British Consulate,*
*Constantinople.*

[1910.]

MY DEAREST FRANK * :
Here I am—for the next two months at least—very blissful with nothing to do at all except to learn some

* Mr. Frank Savery.

KANDILLI : J. E. FLECKER ON HORSEBACK.

[*To face p.* 6.

KANDILLI : IN THE VILLAGE.

Turkish and law ; no posts being vacant at present. Do write to me. I want to know about that essay—can you do anything with it ? Because if not I think the *English Review* (see new address) would take it like a shot—I've got a little influence there now—and I hope I've got a poem in also.

Had a joyous journey out amid Aegean Isles and all the scenes one used to write rotten poetry about : also met a fair Greek maiden called Hellé, of extraordinary intelligence and taste, knowing all poetry in the world. She took me round Athens, O unfaithful one—for my marriage after many vicissitudes is practically fixed for October, secretly, between ourselves.*

This place, praise God, is not a bit like the Near East Exhibition at Olympia, and all mosques are not really exactly the same. By an extraordinary stroke of luck there is no post vacant, so I have nothing to do for next two months but wander round, take photographs and translate a few bits of Turkish newspaper. There is a fine man called Bullard in the service here. The beauty of the place especially up here on the Bosphorus it would be futile to describe. I go riding this evening and that should be a great thing to do.

Everybody here has seen some history : however stupid they are they have good tales to tell and by God it's better to be here than to be wandering about London drawing rooms a sort of aimless literary blood. Still I am unhappy when I think of those two good towns, Oxford and Cambridge, and of many good friends. Am I never to see you again, O Frank ? Write to me, for most pleasant it is to be written to, voyons.

Yours ever,
JAMES.

* The poet was then more or less engaged to a lady in England. Some months later the engagement was broken by mutual consent.

> *The British Consulate,*
> *Cple.*
> *Aug. 2.* [1910.]

MY DEAREST FRANKO :

You of all people telling me to be decadent—you the healthy-minded man !

I am now in charge of about £8,000, all accounts and all archives in the consulate. Pretty hard work . . . I am getting rather stupid. A motor bus here with Marble Arch and Cricklewood inscribed inside it made me feel quite homesick the other day—I am writing in prose about them. I have written one poem, not good enough to copy and send you. . . . Have just finished *Beauchamp's Career* and find it simply splendid—one of his best. Wish I had the rewriting of it in decent English.

So you are off again O Frank. I shan't be shifted from here till end of October. Don't know whether I shall marry ; it's more fun really not knowing. This comes by Embassy bag and costs 1*d.*, which is clever.

The subtlety of the motives of speech of Meredith's characters makes one feel quite a coarse common fellow.

'Fraid I am less decadent. Read *Great Expectations* and *Tale of Two Cities* and thought them not only damn good but very subtle in places.

Will hang my room round with purple cloth and take to opium as a remedy.

Passionately,

JAMES.

> *The Cotswold Sanatorium,*
> *near Stroud, Glos.*
> *October 8.* [1910.]

MY POOR, DEAR WANDERING FRANKO :

I have left the purple East owing to incipient and not too serious comsumpers and having been all but ship-

VIEW OF PRINKIPO
FROM HALKI.

FOUNTAIN IN
STAMBOUL.

[*To face p.* 8.

wrecked in the Mediterranean am safely ensconced beneath the insufficient shelter of this cold and draughty place, seven miles from the maternal and paternal eye. Later I shall go South, I hope to Sicily, and may be able to go with my Greek poetess of whom I told you. And the Freeman is coming to visit me to-morrow. And I'm much better, and shall be able to do some writing, so I'm damned if I see why I should care, so long as I'm on full pay. But I wish there were some one here who wasn't either a tout or else godlessly dull.

I will send you my book on the *Education of the Young*, of which I have just corrected the final proofs.

I am going to write some horrible poems about consumps and a book about poetry.

Dent's may take my novel; they are going to send some suggestions for revising it—which by God it needs.

I won't write any more to you, my dear Frank, but do write. What a great age we live in. You know Galsworthy's *Justice* got the prisons reformed. Have you read it? What do you think of that great man, of Arnold Bennett's *Old Wives Tale*, of Conrad, of *Tono-Bungay*. What a great school of novelists, and how the Victorians are outshined. Don't you think so?

Ever yours phthisically,

JAMES.

Got your long letter about [word illegible] and your note with winter address.

*The Cotswold Sanatorium,*
*Stroud* [*probably late* 1910],
*Thursday.*

MY DEAR FRANKO:

Your most welcome letter to hand. I'm glad the *Tramp* are taking your tale; I didn't so much as get an acknowledgment of the story from Goldring, the Editor, to whom I wrote at once, but he is very busy. Yes, I sent the *Old Wives Tale*. Of course he *is* a poor man, you guess rightly ; but there are I believe one or two other things which aren't potboilers.

I liked your horrid story. You do manage to make the Brutality of Existence and of people the background of everything you write, in an amazing way.

I am getting better and better. I am corresponding with three women at once. It's the old game, Franko. The one I love likes me, I like the one who loves me, and the other fascinates and repels me alternate days. I am dreary dead dog sick of this hole : the girl I love has been gone three weeks : she was 19 and lovelier than Helen of Troy. . . . She was not ill but the sister of a girl who was, and the only girl I've ever seen lovelier than mine . . . was her sister G———. God is a brute : she was wretched ill.

I hope to go to Italy soon.

And the result of it all is, O my Franko, that I send you by the same post a poem "Don Juan from the Shadows," which you will see at once is my masterpiece. I can't send you my book on education (*The Grecians*, Dent, 2*s.*), but it is out and you may buy it ; they only sent me four copies.

I wrote "Don Juan," knowing nothing whatever about him : never having so much as read Molière. Now I have read his marvellous play *Don Juan ou le Festin de Pierre* : I am reading all about the legend in a French monograph of enormous length, and O Frank my life's work is decided on—a play on Don Juan, rivalling in aim *Faust* and *Peer Gynt*.

Of course my conception will be modern. I shall portray Don Juan utterly disappointed in his *grande passion* seeking refuge from sickly and decadent despair first in the world and in the passion for humanity and justice, then questioning religion, then ordinary morality, until finally he becomes an utter sadist. Then

10

comes the statue, which is the miracle, to make him doubt reason itself, and he dies bravely.

I doubt very much if I can do anything so big as this. But I am sick of writing little petty lyrics. When I read immortal stuff like Browning I am miserable, thinking of the poverty of my language and ideas. Think of Love among the Ruins, Up in a Villa down in a City, the Bishop ordering his tomb, praying for horses for his sons and " mistresses with great smooth marbly limbs " —or the poet in Valadolid, Jack is so fond of.

Doing the King's work all the dim day long.

I hope I may see you soon for I shall want help in this enormous undertaking.

Write about *Don Juan* by return if you can.

Ever your old friend,

JAMES.

Flecker arrived in Paris early in January and immediately decided, in spite of contrary advice, not to go to Switzerland, but to stay there and work at *Don Juan*. He was soon settled in rooms near the Etoile and working hard at a large table in a diminutive sitting-room, except for some hours daily of outdoor exercise, long walks in the Bois or the environs.

I remember a visit to Versailles which we made together on a fine frosty afternoon. He had just been reviewing Monypenny's *Life of Disraeli* and was very much thrilled by his subject. I recall him walking with his large strides among statues and fountains, looking neither right nor left and speaking with great animation of the wonderful prospects of politics and how he would like one day to follow the same career as Disraeli and become a great Liberal leader. As Mr. Goldring remarks in his *Life*, the poet was far from indifferent to politics ; the Shelleyan spirit had greatly influenced him, yet being much less " inhuman " than Shelley he probably could never have taken his dearest theories too seriously.

During those weeks in Paris he wrote the beautiful " Epithalamion," which he afterwards placed in *Don Juan*, and besides his work on this play he polished the " Ballad of Iskander " and wrote the " Princess " after a Greek folk-song. In February he went back to England staying successively at Oxford, Cambridge, and London, and returned to Paris early in March on his way to the East.

This second voyage out was not as cheerful as the

ATHENS AND HYMETTUS FROM THE ACROPOLIS.

WHAT WAS LEFT OF THE FRIEZE ON THE PARTHENON BY LORD ELGIN.

[*To face p.* 12.

first one. At the bottom of his heart he dreaded returning to the spot where he had first had the revelation of disease. He felt homesick and depressed and caught a slight cold at Marseilles. Passing Cape Malea he wrote me a long letter asking me to come to Athens and be his wife, for he could not face the idea of living in the East alone. I was to lose no time, to wire my answer to Constantinople and to set out immediately. This letter, which I did not expect, disturbed me greatly, for I had never contemplated the possibility of marrying him, though I admired him for his talent and great intelligence.* Besides, I had to look after my mother, whose state of health was giving signs of serious trouble. She was then living with my brother, who, after resigning from the Greek diplomatic service, had taken a post in a French bank in Paris. My brother promised to look after my mother. She, dear soul, assured me she would bear the separation bravely for my sake. Flecker's first letter was followed by several others at close intervals, urging me to make haste, and announcing he was going to be sent to Smyrna, where as soon as he arrived he would hunt for a small cottage by the sea. He characteristically asked at the end of this letter, " Shall I get a servant, a piano and a bed ? "

I left Paris with my mother and brother, and on reaching Athens I heard that Flecker's health was again giving him trouble. He took a month's leave and arrived in Athens a week after me, looking well enough except for hoarseness, which occurred regularly every evening and worried him a good deal. Following my advice, he went to live at Cephissia, the summer resort of Athens, which at that season was a real paradise of flowers and scents. He spent long hours under the pines breathing that light air of Attica, scented with the thyme

* I remember Flecker when I first met him was very fond of quoting the lines :

Time turns the old days to derision,
Our loves into corpses or wives.

and cytisus in flower and enjoying the walks we took in the evening. The memory of a sunset seen from " My Cephisian window high and cool " is recalled in his " Ode to Hellas."

He was soon feeling quite well again and we were married at Athens on May 25th, in spite of the old Greek belief which considers May an unlucky month. We then stayed at Old Phaleron for a fortnight in a breezy hotel by the sea, where at night the wind blowing in from the four tall French windows looking on to a balcony on the sea-front swept through our bedroom in such gusts that the long curtains 12 feet high flapped all over the place and beat us out of our beds. We then understood the old Italian woman's famous objection to open windows at night—" I don't go to bed to breathe, but to sleep."

The spring was particularly cool that year, so that Phaleron was not yet invaded by its summer crowds ; we had the place all to ourselves and could enjoy some nice lazy walks along the shore and now and then a sail out towards Aegina or Salamis. One day my husband planned a trip by steamer through the Straits of Euboea, and the next morning we embarked at Pireus on one of the many small steamers that carry for a few drachmas a motley crowd of humans, animals and vegetables to and from the innumerable islands and intricate coasts of the Archipelago. Some years before the rival companies running such steamers had grown so numerous that the fares had fallen to nought—it was then said that the agent of a new line offered not only a free passage to Andros, but, moreover, a dish of pilaff to entice passengers hesitating between several boats leaving at the same time for the same destination.

We stayed two days at Chalcis, where we admired the only show of a tide to be found in the Eastern Mediterranean. It is marked by a strong current running in and then out of the narrow Straits of Euripos between

NAUPLIA, BURGI ISLAND : VIEW OF THE MOUNTAINS OF ARGOLIS.

AEGINA : THE PORT.

*[To face p.* 14.

Euboea and the mainland, and makes Chalcis feel more lively. We heard gruesome tales of usurers from one of their victims—the fisherman who rowed us out in his boat at sunset. His grim story was told with a contained hatred expressed in his whole countenance that greatly impressed Roy, to whom I translated the tale, as he could not follow the man's colloquial style. " See that house ? " He pointed to a fine red villa among a cluster of pines on a headland, " built by one of them. Do you know what that man said to me once when I complained I couldn't feed the children and wife ? ' Why do you smoke ? ' he said, ' tobacco costs money.' ' You're no christian,' I said to him, ' to tell a man who's starving to stop smoking.' He looked at the house and spat in the water, then turning to me: " A man like me if I can't smoke might as well be dead, and he said don't smoke, curse him. But then the punishment of God ; he fell ill and rotted away, they buried him piece by piece in his grave ; first one leg, then his arms, then the other leg, so that only the trunk was left for the priest."

He lit one more cigarette and went on grumbling out the misery of the poor and the insolence of the rich, but we were looking at the sunset and following the great wings of light that carried away one more golden day.

We left Chalcis in the morning, and after passing Aedipso and its sulphur springs that throw their boiling, yellow waters into the sea, the steamer crossed over to the mainland. Late in the afternoon we entered the Gulf of Stylis in time to witness a magnificent sunset behind the mountains of Thermopylae, that stood ink-black on a flaming sky. My husband was so taken by the beauty of that landscape and the freshness and verdure of Stylis that he insisted on spending the night on the spot in spite of contrary advice. A rich farmer who had travelled with us on the boat addressed me in the usual familiarly paternal way of Greek peasants, and on hearing our decision of passing the night at Stylis was much alarmed—probably fearing the impression which a " European " foreigner would carry away after such an experience. " Tell the gentleman," he said to me insistently, " that this is no place for you to stop at ; there is only a tavern in Stylis, while if you like to come with me I am taking a carriage to Lamia—that is a town where you have a decent hotel."

A splendid full moon was now shining on the waters, and veils of silver vapour were turning Stylis into a land of fairies, while in the tall poplars by the road a nightingale rippled out his song. My husband would not hear of the farmer's proposal, so we started out to find the wine-shop or tavern that was to provide us with a shelter for the night. It was a most primitive place with a floor of beaten earth, some tables and stools and a few barrels of wine against the walls. The landlord was amiable, but looked uncomfortably shy when we spoke of a room for the night. " I suppose you would prefer two beds in the front room," he said, when we had found the back room he showed us too stuffy. We immediately answered we would rather have the eight beds of the front room, so as not to have other people sharing the room with us. He then picked out two of the beds, which he declared he had cleaned the day before, brought a jug of water and a basin which he placed on the unique chair and carefully shutting the two tiny windows, he departed wishing us " Kalinykta." Our first move was to open the windows ; the room being over the shop there was an uncomfortable smell of cheese and dry fish. Outside, the moonlight was weaving its spells over a wonderful landscape enlivened by the song of the most melodious nightingales I have ever heard, even in Greece, while all the varieties of flower scents perfumed the cool, damp air. But soon myriads of hideous insects were crawling over the walls, the beds were alive with enemies, while an ever louder buzz told us of the invasion of innumerable mosquitoes from which no flight was possible. Armed with a towel we sat on the chair or paced the floor in agony the whole of that memorable night. In the morning we crawled to the shore, and, hailing a boatman, we had a sail in the gulf.

In spite of fatigue, we could not take our eyes off the splendid view of sea and mountains bathed in the morning light. Roy was in high spirits and tried to joke in broken Greek with the old boatman. He afterwards remembered when he received a letter from Rupert Brooke, with a postscript on the way to treat wives, that the same advice had been offered to him by that cheerful old Stylis boatman.*

* [Brooke's letter.]

Surrey, *April*, 1912.

*I*, as an other poet once, have fallen on the thorns of life and bled bucketsfull and I am far too poor to give you the copy of my poems you indecently ask for. Damn you, go down to your local Bowes and Bowes, and order it, and have the cost put down to the Government, like a gentleman and a ProConsul.

Also I do not like the book. It is misprinted, and it recalls the Golden days before the Crash.

Oh, yes : the crash came. Precisely at the beginning of this year. I'd galloped down hill for months, and then nine days I lay without sleep or food. Monsters of the darkest Hell nibbled my soul. They nibbled it away, and therein that noblest part of it which men name the intellect. I am sodden and soft and dead, a don, but less learned, a dotard, but less energetic. I almost write prose-poems. Since January the ninth (portentous date) I have been forbidden to work or run. I drift from place to place and eat enormously and sleep. I am utterly degraded, and shall never climb from this morass. Why has God thus visited me ? I am going to Germany (where my kind abounds) in a day or two. Thence . . . into the Ewigkeit. If you see, any day, marching into the great portals of Beyrout, a fat bald man, with a slobbered red beard and a scaly eye, put him in some quiet asylum for it will be me. I have obtained a divorce from my Muse (the decree is shortly to be made absolute) : she is thought, moreover, to have committed some slight bigamy. I live on stout and modern English fiction. Among toads I am a very hodmandod.

You are married. Why are you married ? Never mind, you will be dead soon. And why do the Italians shoot at you so ? I saw it all in *The Times*. Perhaps you are dead already.

My swarthy friend, Elroy my golden-tongued and lax-metred Orpheus, you would never let me teach you how to write Poetry, but it does not matter now : and you are a fine fellow. When you read in the *East Levant Gazette* that I've taken the last step, weep once, and then lay up the whole thing (with the moral) in your heart, and tell it often to the young. What the moral *is* I shall not tell you. But you may warn them never to be good *and* wise. It does not pay.

Pray for me,
thine RUPERT.

Felicitate your wife from me : but beat her less worse befall.

Our next halting place was Livadia, a quaint little town at the foot of the Helicon. A cheerful stream comes down the main street, and was used to turn the mills of cotton weavers in olden days. The mills are now stilled and the green water runs clear and singing on its bed of cobbles along the pink and white houses. The noise of the babbling waters, so rarely to be heard in Greece, delighted my husband and made him suffer stoically the lack of comfort of our quarters at the small hotel. There at least sleep was possible. I had some quinine, having had a touch of fever, owing probably to the devouring mosquitoes of Stylis, and gave Roy some, preventively.

The next morning we went out for our breakfast, the hotel being what is called in Greece ΞΕΝΟΔΟΧΕΙΟΝ ΥΠΝΟΥ, or sleeping hotel, and providing no food, and found the restaurant or rather tavern to which we were directed had a wooden balcony at the back overhanging a precipice with a fine view over the green plantations of cotton and rice. My husband immediately insisted on our frugal breakfast of black coffee and bread being served on this balcony ; between its disjointed planks, one had giddy glimpses of the deep gorge below, but the proprietor assured us it would hold our weight. Later we went for a walk, and came upon a narrow pass enclosed by tall walls of rock. We were admiring the beautiful hues, blue, red, and gold which coloured those rocks when we were accosted by a man, who said : " You are looking for the Trophonius Sanctuary which I have discovered, it is here on the right." To our confusion we had to confess we were not looking for Trophonius, of whom we both had a dim recollection, and, further, that we had no Pausanias with us, which facts seemed to fill the little man with amazement. We were told he had spent all his small fortune and most of his life searching for this " andron." He had at last found a narrow hole in the rocks leading into a vast subterranean cavern which he maintained was the once famous Trophonius sanctuary mentioned by Pausanias. In spite of our vague notions about his hero, we were soon good friends with the amateur archæologist, who invited us to an after lunch coffee at the central caféneion, and, telling us the pathetic story of his life-long research and the indifference of the Archæological Society of Athens, who refused all help, he begged us to intercede on behalf of Trophonius in high quarters.

Next morning, on leaving Livadia, we had one of our most dramatic adventures. We were to have several such in our future travels, owing chiefly to my husband's dearly cherished principle that one ought never to return from a trip with more than a penny in one's pocket. On preparing to pay the bill he discovered that what he had thought to be a one hundred drachma note in his purse was in reality a ten drachma note. However fantastically cheap hotels and railway fares were in those pre-war days in Greece, ten drachmas really seemed an impossible sum with which to face a two nights' hotel bill and a ten-hours' train journey to Athens. After thoroughly discussing the situation, we decided there was no way out of it. So after paying the bill and giving a sixpence to the boy servant, who expressed his surprise and grateful thanks, and paying the carriage a six-mile drive to the station, our joint purses contained one drachma, with which Roy bought cigarettes to soothe the feelings of outraged railway officials, as we were to travel without tickets. Roy wore his most ingratiating smile when the first official came round, and spoke his best Greek. They were soon three in our carriage discussing this very unusual case, and whether we ought not to be deposited at the first stop. In those days foreigners were few in Greece and not of the ordinary tourist type, so that they generally inspired confidence and respect. Owing to this *rara avis* quality we were allowed to proceed on the assurance that when in Athens we would

19                                                    c 2

leave a splendid camera, which formed the only impressive item amongst our bags, at the station as security.

By the beginning of June we left Phaleron for Corfu, where we had decided to spend the three months' leave generously granted by the F.O. Our boat left Pireus early in the morning, and, going through the Corinth Canal, reached Patras at sunset. While admiring the magnificent view of the Panachaicon and far mountains of Elis gilt in the setting light, Roy discovered that he was no longer wearing a red leather belt which he had purchased at Livadia and which was decorated with small pockets in which he insisted on carrying our money. The beauty of the sunset was greatly overshadowed by this painful incident, which, like all losses, was chiefly annoying because out of a sense of duty one thinks oneself obliged to make some sort of research. Our story seemed to draw no pity either from the captain or the passengers ; only a pretty girl of eighteen or so, whose beautiful dark eyes expressed the truest sympathy when she heard my husband was a poet, insisted that poets were bound to be careless and lose their purses, which made Roy smile and forget his worry.

We arrived in Corfu penniless, save for a sum which was in my trunk in the hold and could not be got at. The hotel porter fortunately turned up on board and paid our bill (food and drink being charged apart from passage-fares on Greek lines). We stayed four or five days at the St. George Hotel ; the first two my husband was not at all well and had to keep quiet. When he felt better we drove about in quest of a small house, and were lucky enough to find a four-roomed cottage in a large garden on the Canoni road. The day we moved into it there was a deluge, the rain falling in sheets, shutting out the view, and turning the garden into a swamp. We felt thoroughly miserable that first evening amid the howling of the wind and the torrents of water in that cheerless whitewashed dining room lighted by two candles, the neighbouring grocer not being able to supply petroleum for our lamps. But next morning the sun shone in the purest of skies, the birds sang wildly, and the garden leaves seemed varnished and lacquered in brilliant green. And such scents were swept in by the breeze! Our only troubles during those two months were the flies by day and the mosquitoes at night, and the inevitable lamb chop for lunch and dinner. Whatever meat was ordered from the town butcher it always turned out to be lamb chops when delivered. Fortunately, now and then we were awakened at sunrise by some fisherman brandishing a large lobster or a silvery fish at our bedroom window. My husband soon gained weight and felt much stronger, though he was often restless for lack of intelligent society. He as yet had never experienced solitude, having always lived in a congenial scholarly atmosphere, surrounded by friends who admired him, or whom he admired. Though we had many tastes in common, and even, I may say, affinities, in those days I lacked the high spirits I am often capable of raising now that I am older and wiser, having faced and left behind many troubles which then I only dimly foresaw. In youth the shadow of the future has for us a more perturbing influence than immediate reality. We then believe we ought to fight and conquer fate, and instead of trying to get through as best we can we strive to clear our path of thorns. Realising the inanity of our efforts, we then fret and charge ourselves, when the only thing would be to face necessity with the spirit of the ephemera, dancing away their short hour in a ray of sunlight.

In a fit of this restlessness, my husband thought of going to Italy, and we decided for Siena, but the mood changed soon. He set to writing, which he had not done since leaving Smyrna, and wrote some of his best poems, and also began again working at his Turkish, so that

Italy was forgotten, and we stayed where we were. The heat was now great, but not unbearable when one could avoid all effort during the midday hours. The mornings were delightful in the garden under the tall orange trees, and the sunsets an ever-renewed splendour. He would lean on the low wall that edged the end of the garden, where the view extended far over the olive groves across the road to the west and watch the pageant of the departing god ; or we would walk to the headland overlooking a large sea-lake or lagoon, where the most wonderful iridescent colours were reflected. In the morning he used to work in the garden.

Monotony was broken now and then by long drives to many pleasant spots on the hills or by the sea. One such excursion which particularly enchanted the poet was a long drive across the island to the monastery of Palaeokastritsa. The monastery consists of a simple chapel and some small buildings for the monks surrounding it, the whole whitewashed. It stands like a small citadel on a high, rocky headland about a hundred feet above the sea, united to the land by a narrow strip of rock. The terrace that runs round the buildings commands an extensive view over the western sea towards Italy. The egoumenos, or prior, showed us with pride a trellised vine spread on the eastern side of the terrace affording blue shade for the idle noonday hours. My husband's camera raised the hopes of the community who posed before it with delight and were promised copies of their portraits. A lay-brother, who herded the goats outside the monastery walls, was a particularly picturesque figure and greatly amused us. He was short, with a very large Caliban head, his hair forming a huge grey puff-ball on the top of which stood the diminutive black monastic cap. He wore an extremely short cassock, green with age, scarcely reaching below the knees, under which showed a no longer white kilt or fustanella and the usual woollen gaiters and bare

CORFU : MOUSE ISLAND.

THE LITTLE
MONASTERY ON THE
OTHER ISLET.

[To face p. 22.

feet of the shepherds. His photo, as well as those of the other monks, was not to come to light, the plates we had purchased in Corfu the day before proving to have been years old, so that all that series came to nothing. We were sorry to disappoint our models, and remembered how eagerly in their loneliness they had accepted a newspaper which we chanced to have and gave them. Cut off from the world and leading a life of contemplative idleness, which must soon stop all activity of the mind, they yet do not seem to attain easily that state of earthly detachment which is the ideal norvana of monastic life.

Another charming excursion I remember to the mountain village of Péléka, but there our enjoyment was marred by the persecutions of the otherwise pleasing-to-look-at village children. While the younger of the band were easily persuaded by our coachman to return to their homes and leave us to lunch in peace on a high spot in the pine woods above, one young rascal about fifteen, looking like a young satyr, in spite of his graceless clothes and battered straw hat, proved to be implacable. He worried us by mocking us from behind the trees, either imitating our talk like a parrot or whistling in a most irritating manner. At last my husband, losing his temper, took up his heavy stick and chased him back into the wood. This only drove away the wretch for a short while, and just as Roy had produced from his pocket a book of Italian verse—I believe Carducci—and begun reading aloud, the mocking-bird was again heard close at our elbow. People with sensitive nerves are made unhappy by incidents of this sort. Yet the splendour of clouds and mountains and laughing seas are only for them—the clowns that torment them have no use for the beauty of the world.

Some Athenian friends to relieve our solitude had sent us an introduction to a Corfiote gentleman, who, besides a candle and nail factory, also possessed a model farm which provided us with scarce but excellent fresh butter for our tea and breakfast. This worthy man was the kindest and most obliging of humans, and thought himself bound to take us for a drive in his car, providing us with what in those parts of the world was a magnificent meal. From the high spot to which he took us we had a wonderful view over the Pantocrator and the Mountains of Epiros across the sea, and the meal under the pines was heartily enjoyed, but the man was so excessively dull, taking no interest in any possible topic, not even business or politics (a rare specimen in Greece), that the task of avoiding long silences, which in all countries but England are considered by polite people a fearful calamity to be fought by all means, was very fatiguing and quite overcame me. This unsuccessful effort at sociability stopped us from any further attempts at exploration of Corfiote society.

Sea-bathing we had not much of ; the sea was some distance from the cottage, and the sunny road to it was to be avoided for Roy's health. On the last attempt we bathed at a rocky beach where the sea was particularly clear over a bed of seaweed, and there my husband lost his ring, an old Greek intaglio which had belonged to my grandfather, showing a figure of Demeter holding a pomegranate cut in red cornelian. He spent a long time searching for it in the lapis lazuli waters, but without avail, and I believe that from that day he kept a grudge against the sea and bathed no more.

Sailing was another of our ambitious attempts, a difficult enterprise in those parts, the wind being most unsteady, and the many headlands causing sudden gusts and not less sudden dead calms. We once had the luck of finding a small white cutter belonging to some club, and my husband immediately decided to set off for the day. Having doubled the cape that extends to the north of the town with a fair breeze, we suddenly entered a dead calm, and after waiting about for a while had to sit

to the oars. There was a swell, which had not been notice-
able as long as the boat went at a fine pace, but once it
was still I soon felt badly upset, while my husband, who
was a much better sailor, tried to cheer me up, assuring
me there was nothing like rowing to cure sea-sickness.
The boat was a fairly large one ; we could only pull
one oar each and that a heavy one. We rowed wearily
in the heat of a fine breathless day for five hours and got
back about sunset. Next time we went out with that
boat we had a sailor who knew something of the game
of the winds.

By the second half of August we had to say good-bye
to Phaeacia with a heavy heart and a grateful one for
the many beautiful hours it had given us and its bene-
ficial influence on my husband's health, which seemed at
the time perfectly restored. We then thought we were
leaving for Smyrna, which we were not to see again, and
made plans accordingly. As for our departure, the
inevitable contrary incidents which always seemed to
occur when we were to travel from one place to another
did not spare us and made it a very dramatic affair. In
accordance with my husband's principles we had just
enough pennies left when the day came, but not one
penny too much, so that the last interview with our
rather screechy landlady turned out to be a painfully
noisy one, and the carriage that had been ordered to
fetch us never turned up in time, while the terrible landlady added to our nervous anxiety. The price of insigni-
ficant utensils that had suffered at our hands was fiercely
discussed, but as we could not afford to part even with
a farthing we could only refuse to pay very reasonable
damages amounting to something like three shillings,
and she was threateningly told to send on her complaint
to the British Consulate at Smyrna. This solution was
not much to her taste, and she consequently put on a still
more forbidding attitude.

In the meanwhile a carriage passed and was called to

take us to the small pier, from which a boat was to row us to the harbour, some three miles away. The coach-man proved to be one of those unfortunate wretches who are sent to work in Corfu for the sake of the climate. He was terribly weak and emaciated, and pathetically eager to lift the bags and things, not to be thought a dying man. I shall never forget the nightmare of that face, which at the time made me feel quite ill. At last we got away from the irate landlady and the lachrymose servant Maria, but on reaching the pier we found that a large trunk containing our most precious possessions had been left behind. My husband had to go back for it, and to his horror he saw the landlady sitting on it. However, he looked at her so fiercely that she made no resistance, and we were at last off with our five trunks and innumerable small luggage. We were afraid of missing the steamer, when on reaching the harbour, our boatmen were stopped and told they had no right to bring passengers from other parts of the island by sea, thus taking work out of the hands of the regular harbour boatmen. We had the greatest difficulty in persuading the port officials that we knew nothing of these regula-tions and could not be made to lose our steamer by our boatmen's fault. We at last got on board in a state of utter exhaustion at the very last moment, to find that no berths were available, and that we should have to pass the night in a sort of smoking-room on deck. Fortunately the passage was a good one and we both slept in spite of our hard narrow couches, though my sleep was troubled by dragons sitting on my chest and trains rushing past and falling into the sea, vague reminiscences of the emotions of the day or forebodings of further adventures.

We found Athens overcome by a heat wave ; the thermometer rising to 110 in the shade we were forced to few and slow movements in our preparations for the journey to Smyrna. Then my husband having one

morning called at the Legation for his passport found a
F.O. wire, telling him to proceed to Beyrut to act as
V.Consul there. A few days later we sailed from
Pireus on a little white, very swift, Greek boat, which
was to take us in thirty-eight hours to Alexandria. The
heat was awful, and we were very grateful to the captain
who ordered the meals to be served on deck. My
husband was in high spirits in spite of the torrid air and
waved a cheerful good-bye to Athens when we moved
out of the Pireus harbour and saw the Acropolis fading
away in a pale mauve mist.

On the second night we caught a glimpse of the
southern coast of Crete, or rather of a few spare lights
showing it was there, and about noon the second day
the tall Alexandria lighthouse appeared and told us we
had reached the flat coast of Egypt. In spite of the heat
Roy decided we should have a look at Cairo and go on to
Port Said by train, to find there a boat for Beyrut.

And now another dramatic departure was in store
for us. Having been to the Consulate to greet the
V.Consul, whom my husband knew, and have our
passports stamped, we were told to hurry up or we should
lose the Cairo train. The coachman whipped up his
horses and off we went full speed and were nearly at the
station when Roy discovered that his wallet was no
longer in his pocket. He shouted to the coachman to
return to the Consulate, where it had been left. Fortunately no sooner had he turned his horses than we saw
a mounted cawass galloping in our direction and waving
the precious wallet in his hand. The train was just
moving off when we scrambled in and fell back in our
seats utterly exhausted with the heat and excitement.
We were soon aroused from our torpor by the unusual
sight of a tall white sail that seemed to glide and cut its
way through the high reeds in the fields along the line.
It was soon doubled by another, shaped like a large
butterfly, and we then knew they were following the

27

intricate maze of invisible canals that cut across the level Delta plain.

The journey to Cairo is fortunately a short one, for the temperature in the carriages seemed to rise ever higher as we were going inland. The tall shady room of the Cairo hotel seemed to us a real oasis when we reached it in the blazing heat of the August noon. My husband was delighted to be in Egypt in the hottest season when the place is empty of tourists and most foreigners, and shows its most characteristic aspect. He was now more obedient to the local way of dealing with the heat and would not have attempted to see the pyramids at 2 p.m. We only ventured out about sunset and drove to see the Sphinx; as the snapshots taken by my husband show, we were alone there, thanks to the season, but the bodyguard that follows all tourists in those regions was there ready for the pose and as absurdly picturesque as ever.

The sunset was a lurid one with a bright orange and green sky, just as on Cook's posters, but the stillness of the desert and that sense of tragic desolation that falls suddenly with the gathering darkness, the inhuman form of the Sphinx taking on a truly formidable aspect, is not to be found on posters. We both felt intensely a sort of sacred horror and were glad to be driving back along the dusty road to Cairo and the noises of life.

On the third day we left for Port Said to take the boat for Beyrut. We then saw for the first time a real mirage from the train. We were prosaically seated in the dining car having lunch, when my husband looking out of the window said to me: " I wonder what town that can be." Taking up my glasses I followed his gaze and saw quite clearly domes, minarets and a few palms, and wondered too, when our neighbour—an Anglo-Egyptian—turned to us and said, " There's no town there, you are only seeing a mirage." Looking out we saw the perspective had already changed; a large lake

CAIRO:
A PYRAMID
AND OUR ESCORT.

CAIRO:
COURTYARD
OF A
MOSQUE.

CAIRO:
DOOR OF THE
CITADEL-MOSQUE.

[*To face p.* 28.

bordered with groups of palms had replaced the phantom town.

Our arrival at Beyrut was, as usual, marked by incidents—tragi-comic ones in this case. We were expecting to be met by the usual gold-braided official, the cawass so indispensable to the prestige of Europeans in the pre-war East. Seeing no one was awaiting us my husband went on shore alone and drove to the Consulate to bring the necessary reinforcement for the landing of our luggage. He returned accompanied by a magnificent, though elderly Druse, as fierce-looking as one could wish, with his large curved sword dangling at his side. No sooner had we landed before the Turkish Customs than a violent quarrel broke out between our man and the Turkish official of the " Régie," who insisted upon searching our trunks and bags to make sure we had no tobacco. Selim could not allow such a breach in the diplomatic conventions and we suddenly saw the Turk jump up and seize him by the throat while the eyes of the unfortunate cawass naturally large and prominent, seemed to burst out of his head like a lobster's. We sprang to the rescue, and my husband managed to separate the two infuriated men, and then we all had to proceed and interview the head of the Customs, an important Turkish official. My French being handy I had to tackle the Osmanli who, though polite was, one could see, deeply disgusted, like all Orientals, at having to discuss with a female. Nevertheless, we gained our point, and the irascible " Régie " man was ordered to make amends and to kiss Selim ! Turning round we saw the two recent enemies locked in a tight embrace.

Hot and excited, we now decided, following Selim's suggestion, to take the train to the Lebanon and stop at a hotel at Aley ; the Consul-General was staying near there until November. The train left from the quays before the Customs, and we soon found it was full and that there was no first-class carriage. My husband seeing a man with a fez who bustled round, and thinking he was the train conductor, asked him if he could not have a carriage added for British officials. The man answered it was too late, the train would be leaving, that he could do nothing. At which my husband being tired and impatient called him a dirty Turk who wanted Bakshish. Then the little man flew into a rage, shouted that he was the station master and a better Christian than " vous Monsieur," and that he would send in a complaint to the Consulate against my husband, who had treated him like a dog, etc., etc. We were thoroughly annoyed and I did my best to soothe the man's ruffled feelings, arguing that my husband, speaking a foreign language had used words much too strong for his meaning, begging him to accept our apologies for the " malentendu." After fussing for a while he was calmed, and went so far as to order a first-class carriage to be added for Aley.

But our tribulations were not yet ended. With us in the carriage sat a Syrian from Egypt, who on the way up showed us some plantations of young maritime pines along the line, insisting they were cedars, of which we could not be convinced. Then he went on to praise the hotel at Aley at which his family were staying, exalting the excellence of the cooking and the hospitality of the owner. Having no other information on the place we decided to go there. The heat being great, a damp clammy heat, we were looking forward to the cool rest in a shady lounge. But the much-praised hotel proved to be a dismally, uncomfortable native sort of Caravanserai with rows of small bedrooms built round a central courtyard, the ascetic plank beds covered with a scanty native coverlet and no sheets, the whole picturesque enough in its way, but according very little solace to the weary traveller. My husband was so depressed at the prospect and at the sight of the terrible food that was offered us, and we were both so exhausted that we lay face downwards on our scanty beds and sobbed out our misery.

Relieved after this outburst I then decided there must be a better hotel in the place and that we ought to find out. My husband went to explore and soon returned in triumph, saying he had found a very nice-looking hotel facing the station. Thither we immediately repaired and found decent quarters where we stayed for about two months, while the great heat made Beyrut intolerable. At the back of the hotel was a pine wood stretching over the hills, from which in the late afternoon we used to watch the magnificent sunsets over the sea, and the blue mists in the deep valleys below us rise with the night. As always in the mountains, the night seemed to creep up from the depths, while the peaks above, crowned with tall rocks, were still violently flushed by the rays of the setting sun.

By the end of October we had found comfortable quarters in the annexe of the German Hotel at Beyrut. Our sitting-room looked out on to the sea-front, and I remember we often used to watch an old man who under the scorching sun stood in the shallow water, a dark skeleton bent with age, mysteriously absorbed in sifting water. In reality he was sifting the sand for gold. Stooping, he filled his sieve and shook it in cadence hour after hour, carefully examining its contents for particles of the precious metal. Another interesting sight which we enjoyed from those windows was the bath of a camel which was now and then brought to enter the water with many a grunt and shake of hump. Camels are always interesting and original in their movements; my husband watched on the Damascus road one day the rare sight of a camel going mad with rage, dancing on its four legs a sort of jig before its terrified driver, shaking off one by one from its back the heavy oil tins with which it was laden, that went rolling down the uneven cobbles of the steep road.

November was still fine and warm, and we could enjoy afternoon walks in the Lebanon, or by the sea, and some rides on the large expanse of sands stretching to the north-east along the coast. The flowery valley of the Nahr-el-Kelb or Dog River was also a favourite spot. One day walking by this river, which was swollen by the rains, we ventured on the low wall that separated its bed from a narrow canal that ran along it. This wall, about 2 feet wide, stood about three or four above the water, and when I had gone on it about 100 yards I suddenly felt the rushing water on my right and the glitter of the canal on my left made me giddy. I sat down abruptly, declaring I could go no further. To my astonishment my husband who was preceding me and seemed to walk quite unconcerned, answered back that he also felt queer. I simply crawled back on all fours and did not look round, but I suspected my husband of having adopted the same undignified but safe attitude. Fortunately the wilderness round was complete, or the Consular prestige might have suffered from such an ignominious retreat.

In December the short Syrian rain-season set in. The rain came in heavy downpours, stopping all out-of-doors life and turning the streets of Beyrut into rivers of slime. Now and then the low ceiling of clouds would be rent and the hot rays of the sun would stream through, sucking the damp in heavy mists. The time of social life came with the winter and we made several acquaintances among the Consular and local society, not devoid of charm. Several interesting people, too, turned up now and then, interesting sometimes owing to their personalities, but more often owing to the singular "relief" they acquired when placed against the foreign background, giving us some very vivid pictures of cranky humanity. Late in

December it was decided we should spend Christmas at Damascus.

Unfortunately it rained during the three days of our stay there, consequently our impression of Damascus was not that of the Arabs, who call it the Garden of Eden. At the hotel where we stopped we were glad to find a young English officer from India and his wife. My husband had met him at Beyrut some weeks before and they had remembered having been together at Uppingham. This Mr. P. was studying Arabic, and both he and his wife being Anglo-Indians were great linguists in Hindustani and several Indian dialects. Together with this charming pair we paid our visit to the British Consul, an old acquaintance, for he had been a passenger on the *Crimée* a year before when we had first met, my husband and I, and had been one of the party to Athens. He was a strange person and very much disliked and calumniated by the British Colony for his un-British lack of decorum. He had lived something like twenty years as Vice-Consul at Jeddah, which may have had something to do with his loss of social prejudices. In that infernal hole of a place he had married an Italian singer, who may have been an excellent wife to him, but was not very decorative in the official way and, besides, spoke not a word of English. They were both very fond of animals, and their lumbering old palace of a house was full of cats, dogs, owls, crows, parrots in cages placed along corridors and filling several rooms, besides a funny old ostrich who lived in the porter's lodge in lieu of a porter and poked its silly head at visitors. The smell was awful and took one's breath away on entering this menagerie. The master of the house was to be met roaming about in a labyrinth of unfurnished rooms with his hat on his head, and this hat, a grey felt one, had its brim half separated from the crown, and was in consequence strangely undulated.

I heard the war had driven Mr. D. with his wife, cats,

owls and all back to England, where he lived, and lately died in a small house at Hampstead, far from his romantic Damascene palace; a dismal end for the cranky old gentleman.

That day in Damascus we also met another type of Consul, who had undergone the same demoralising influence of a long residence in the East, and though the effects were different in the case of the Frenchman, yet he also had reached a state of wisdom very near to annihilation, the result of a life spent between Trebizond Mossul and Jeddah with the routine of work and a scanty salary. We had heard the newly arrived French Consul was staying at our hotel and paid him a visit. We were introduced into a stately drawing-room upholstered in bright red plush with canary yellow curtains. In the midst of this striking scenery before a small table sat an oldish man in a black frock coat, the picture of subdued neatness, playing a game of " écarté " with a young person in flame-coloured satin with many gold ornaments over her small body and a pair of very large dark eyes in a shyly smiling face.

We heard from her she was the daughter of the hotel owner, a Greek from Laconia, and came in the afternoons to enliven the solitude of the newly arrived Consul, who seemed very grateful for her broken French and simple talk. This man had given up taking a leave for years, feeling too weary and too uninterested to face his native land's different ways of life. He had lost much but had retained the tidy dullness of the office-trained Frenchman. There was something more romantic and more attractive in his English colleague's unbridled detachment.

A vivid memory of our short Damascus stay is that of an early morning when we both woke up at the sound of a singularly beautiful voice singing in passionate accents the glory of Allah. The voice seemed to come from a dark corner of the room. I rushed to the window and drawing the curtains saw the platform of a minaret not 2 feet away and a muezzin with uplifted head, who was warbling like a nightingale that exalted song. We were told this bird-voiced " singing man " was a devout cobbler of the neighbourhood.

One late afternoon the rain having stopped for a while, we drove out to the old pilgrim's road that leaves the town towards the south. It is now deserted, the pilgrimages proceeding by steamer and train, and the numerous Khans that were grouped in that quarter are crumbling to ruins. We left the carriage and advanced on foot along the desolate kalderim, the mud coming up nearly to the knees. On both sides as far as the eye could reach the muddy track was bordered with rows and rows of thickly set tombs of pilgrims who had fallen on the way, behind them the immensity of the desert spread under a low, lead-coloured sky. Not a shrub or blade of grass, the grey tombstones were crazily aslant in all directions, the stone turbans and fezes crowning them seemed stooping in crowded confusion and whispering old forgotten tales in the wind. The grandeur and desolation made us shudder and we hurried back to the carriage with the night and terror at our heels.

---

Till March 20th
*Hotel Bon Séjour,*
1 *Rue Brey,*
*Paris.*

After—*The British Embassy,*
*Constantinople.*

DEAR FRANK,—in Heaven's name send your address, as I want to send you an enormous long communication and much manuscript.

Yours ever,
JAMES E. FLECKER.

Till March 21st
*Hotel Von Séjour,*
1 *Rue Brey,*
*Paris.*
Afterwards—*The British Embassy,*
*Constantinople.*
*March,* 1911.

MY DEAREST FRANK,

Your mother has just sent me your address which I wrote for, as I was not sure you were still at Munich, so I am sitting down to tell you all about myself and to ask you a great favour.

The Doctor wanted me to stay in the Sanatorium till the end of January, and then to go to Italy, but I determined to amuse myself instead. I have been to Paris, Oxford, Cambridge, London, Paris since Jan. 7th. I am absolutely cured and leave for Constantinople on the 21st on board Paquet steamer. I shall probably be sent to Smyrna next month as acting Vice-Consul. I am better than I have ever been in my life. I weighed 10 stone 5 lbs. when I came to England, now I weigh 12½ stone. Also my poor clothes that I had made when I was well, before leaving for the East for the first time ! I took another lot to be altered here and he had to take out the waistcoat 8 centimetres round the chest, and, alas, 13 centimetres round the belly ! . . .

Now for literature. First of all, Franko, you must know that the hope of the Young Oxford push is the *English Review*, address 11, Henrietta Street, London, W.C., editor Austin Harrison.* The *English Review*

* The *English Review* was founded in the winter of 1908 by Mr. Ford Madox Hueffer, who, with Mr. Douglas Goldring as his sub-editor, made it a literary periodical of remarkable brilliance and solidity, the high standard of which has never been equalled since. A year later, however, the *Review* was bought by Sir Alfred Mond (now Lord Melchett), who installed Mr. Austin Harrison as editor. Under this *régime* the *Review* inevitably became less purely literary, and when the price was reduced to a shilling an attempt was made to capture a wider circulation by an infusion of more political and topical articles ; nevertheless,

for February contained a review by me of Courthope and Symons, two histories of the Byronic movement : 4 guineas. The *English Review* for March contained " The Ballad of Iskander " by me (I am sending you a MS. copy) 9 guineas and sorely needed. The *English Review* for April will contain several poems by one Jack Beazley of whom you may have heard. The *English Review* for May should contain an article on J. C. Snaith's works—he is a very great novelist : read *Broke of Covenden*, and *Wm. Jordan Junior*—which I have been commissioned to undertake, and what is now left of that atrocious poem on Don Juan you so justly censured. I am writing today, Frank, to my friend, Mavrogordato, who reads all the MS. to tell them to look out for contributions from you, they are fond of your sort of writing extremely. Forgot to mention that the *E.R.* for December contained a glowing review of my little book *The Grecians*, A Dialogue on Education, Dent, 2/-, which I don't know if you've seen or heard of yet.

Did that bloody " *Tramp* " pay you ? It has gone bust.

Now I will with cheerful egoism record my late progress.

A. The book of Poems has been transferred to Dent's, who will reissue it, possibly with additions.

B. I wrote in the years of my youth a novel called *The King of Alsander*. I had cheerfully given up all hope of ever getting it published, when suddenly Mavrogordato, that merry Greek to whom I had sent it, tells

---

the *Review* continued to publish work by Hardy, Conrad, Arnold Bennett, George Moore, Walter Sickert, H. G. Wells, Max Beerbohm, W. H. Hudson, Norman Douglas, Robert Bridges, John Masefield, Walter de la Mare, Rupert Brooke and W. H. Davies. Mr. Austin Harrison's sub-editor and literary adviser, to whom some of these letters are addressed, was Mr. John Mavrogordato, who held the post till the autumn of 1912, when he was succeeded by Mr. Norman Douglas. Mr. Mavrogordato had also been till 1911 reader for the publishing firm of J. M. Dent, and it was in that capacity that he first met J. E. Flecker, although he had also read and admired the manuscript of the " Bridge of Fire " when it had been submitted to the firm of Elkin Matthews in June, 1907.

me to take it to one Secker, a publisher. And lo and behold it is accepted for publication on the usual terms, but I am to revise it carefully. Would you could help me, Franko ! It is to be published in January.

C. I accomplished the above two marvels in a ten-days' stay in London, as well as the Snaith article promise and the collecting of the books for it. But I did a more wondrous thing, I finished my play *Don Juan* on Tuesday, revised it Wednesday, had it typed Thursday, gave it to Bernard Shaw to read Friday, got it back with a letter and got a letter to Trench, Lessee of the Hay-market Theatre Monday, sent to it Trench Tuesday, for an appointment with Trench Thursday and found he had read it and went off to Paris the same night.

Bernard Shaw wrote :—" You have great qualities for writing for the stage—some of the highest in fact. One scene (with Tisbea, Act III) is one of the best I have ever read—it is in fact a stroke of genius. I find it difficult to advise you. Your play is too rough for the commercial stage—you should try the Little Theatre " (just what I *won't* do).

Trench said the same thing—but was very flattering and hopeful. " Don't give up writing for the stage," he said : " I will read carefully everything you submit. I can't commission the play from you, but if you revise it—at present it is too *décousu*—I will read it again care-fully. It contains most beautiful poetry."

Not bad for a beginner ! So, Franko darling, will you help me. I send you one of the MS. by same post. Blue Pencil it as much as you like—write suggestions all over it and I will be everlastingly grateful. B. Shaw and Trench are right ; it's too *décousu*—but how can I pull it together ? So write me a letter here just to say you've got the play and then send it to Constantinople about the 28th if you are ready with him. I am already dreaming of other and better plays.

Why do you *never* appear anywhere ? You could

come to Constanti for a fiver, you know. It's years since we've seen each other.

Send something to the *English Review* at once. By the way, if you cared to send the article on me to E. W. Sutton, Worcester Coll. for the *Oxford Magazine*, they would print it but not pay you : the *English Review* have already reviewed me. But a moment's wait till Dent's are out with the new edition !

Ever your devoted,<br>JAMES.

(Written from Constantinople)

MY DEAR FRANK,

I am afraid the *English Review* is no use. It has puffed me already—about 2 pages of laudation in the July number.

Chapman and Hall publish it.

Try *Oxford and Cambridge Review*.

Looking forward to your letter tomorrow. Hope you will be acumin here.

Have been set to work doing accounts ! etc.

JAMES.

*March* 1911.

MY DEAR MAVRO * :

This is a picture of a place where, thank God, I'm not—near Sanatorium. I will send you the MS. from Constantinople : will then need both copies. I have sent three " Don Juan " poems to Harrison, as long as the long one goes in in May I shan't complain if the others are rejected. Secker has sent an agreement form. I shall dedicate the novel to you if I may. I have told my friend, F. Savery, to send some prose to the *English Review*. Will you look 'em over ; they are very good and rather in style I think of the *Review*—trenchant, psychological stories. They will come from Germany.

* Mr. John Mavrogordato.

You are a real angel.  Forgive a p.c. positively too broke with sending MS. about to afford 2½*d*. till a fiver comes from my bank.

Ever yours,

JAMES ELROY FLECKER,

1 rue Brey,

Paris, till 21st.

(Written from Paris.)   (*March* 1911.)

*The British Embassy,*

*Constantinople,*

*Sunday.*

MY DEAREST FRANKO :

Ever so many thanks for your *gentil* telegram.  I leave 22nd from Marseilles : shall arrive Cple, 28th.  Hope to find a goodly enormous epistle from you waiting for me.

Ever yours,

JAMES.

*March* 1911.

*The British Embassy,*

*Constantinople.*

DEAR MAVRO :

Just off from Marseilles.  You promised me Norman Douglas' book to review.  As I am keen on reviewing it, do sent it to Constantinople, and let me find it awaiting me.  Ordinary Constantinople book post.

Ever yours in haste,

JAMES ELROY FLECKER.

*The British Consulate,*

*Smyrna, Asia Minor.*

*Sunday* (*April* 1911.)

MY DEAREST FRANKO :

I am actually writing from Constantinople, but I am just off to the above address, so write to me there in future.  I do not know how to thank you for all the

40

A Fountain in Stamboul.

Constantinople : View of Galata Quays and Tower.

[*To face p.* 40.

trouble you have taken: I shall probably adopt very nearly all your suggestions, but I shall not set to work till I get to Smyrna. Of course I shall send you the revised MS. I am sure your suggestions about leaving out the Owen Jones-Don Pedro scene is a right one. I am very puzzled about Act I : it seems to me to be deadly unstageable, and Bernard Shaw thought so too.

I have another dreadful trial in store. I have got to rewrite that novel of mine for publication. It seems to me that it will be the devil, and in my weakness I long to send it to you.

Now with regard your own work, my dear Franko, your tale *was* published in the *Tramp*, but the forsaken people have gone bust. I thought they had paid you : had I dreamt they had not, I would have screwed some money out of them in London. Write a laconic letter to them saying you might at least have a bound volume of the half year *Tramp*. Your tale was illustrated too. Sorry I should have been responsible for the wasting of it.

The *English Review* takes stories, my son—exactly of your type. Send them to,

> J. Mavrogordato, Esq.,
> *English Review* Offices,
> 11 Henrietta Street,
> Covent Garden, W.C.

He is not the editor, he is on the staff though, and is anxiously awaiting them. You are a blighter; you ought to have sent them long ago. Don't send your only copies as they are apt to lose them. Send two of your best to begin with.

What do you think of *The Ballad of Iskander?* Or had you seen it before.

I am nobly going to do my own work and not pick your brain for ideas about J. C. Snaith. But I should

like to know whether you have read *Broke of Covenden*
and *William Jordan Junior* and what you think of them.

I will not comment on your criticism then, my dear
Franko, but I will revise my play according. I expect I
shall marry my Greek girl soon and live happy ever
afterwards. I am going to Smyrna for 5 months certain,
possibly for 8. It is a jolly place and healthy. If I marry
you must come and see us. . . .

Yours ever, with deep thanks,
JAMES.

*The British Consulate,*
*Smyrna.*
*Wednesday.* (*April* 1911.)

Off to the above address at once, my dear Mavro.
Ever so many thanks for MacKenzie's book; I haven't
yet had Douglas'. I send you Snaith: ram it through
the May number if you can. If Beazley's poems are in
the April number *do* send me a copy. Am going to
marry my Greek poetess just as soon as I can—probably
in about a month. This play has got to be revised up
and down. Would you like to take it to the Little Theatre
people and show it them and see if they want to see the
revise? Let me have Douglas' book to Smyrna: and
let me know what you think of Savery's work if it arrives.
Shall be in Smyrna five months at least.

Wish I had been commissioned to review not so much
*The New Machiavelli* as the ideas in it. But it *is* a great book.

Ever yours,
JAMES ELROY FLECKER.

*British Consulate-General,*
*Smyrna.*
*April* 20*th*, 1911.

MY DEAR MAVRO:

I hope to hear from you soon. I am going to marry
my Greek Poetess Hellé Skiadaressi on the 10th May.

I enclose an amusing article. Will it do for the *Review*? Please tell me how things are going on. I haven't done a thing except Snaith since I left England; my brain is addled. I think the *Review* might like this because it is consistent with the *Review's* policy.

Do let me hear from you soon.

Ever yours,
JAMES E. FLECKER.

*British Consulate-General,*
*Smyrna.*
*April* 21, 1911.

MY DEAREST FRANKO:

Received another letter from you this morning—for which many thanks.

I want to announce formally that provided my health holds out and the Disposer of Events is willing I am going to marry my Greek Poetess on May 15th next instant or whatever it is called.

We would have sent you a beautiful card, but as she is in Paris and I am here it is too hard to arrange these things, so please take this as formal.

I am writing such a lot of these notes that I think I'll stop here. Sorry to hear you sprained your wrist. I'm off writing just now—have not been quite so well lately—but am getting better.

Congratters on being also a servant of the great Government! How I should love to see you again!

JAMES.

Please write,
*Poste Restante,*
*Corfu.*
*June,* 1911.

MY DEAR MAVRO:

Everybody has different criticisms on my play—so I have decided to leave it—but I have altered it a good bit here and there. So let me know what G. Barker thinks and I will send him the new edition. We are off to above address tomorrow. At present we are at old Phalerum. We shall stay at Corfu a month or two. Does the Ed. *English Review* know that all the best men loathe A. C. Benson (very properly) to such an extent that they threaten to give up subscribing. Don't you agree with them and me ? I think he's a ——.

Will write properly from Corfu. Many thanks telegram and letter.

J. E. FLECKER.

*Casa Bogdanos,*<br>
*Stratia,*<br>
*Corfu.*

*Caro Franco mio—me voici, marié, content.* Are you having a holiday soon ? We are either going to stay here (we have hired a cottage) or else going in a fortnight to Italy with designs on Siena. Have revised *Don Juan*, but have not been very obedient. You shall see the copy when typed. We should love to see you, O Franco. My health has improved again. Could you get either here or to Siena in July-August ?

Thine ever,<br>JAMES.

*Casa Bogdanos,*<br>
*Stratia,*<br>
*Corfu.*<br>
*Tuesday.* [*June,* 1911.]

MY DEAR MAVRO :

Forgive this filthy piece of paper—the last scrap I have left—and don't be wrath with me if I exploit you shamelessly—for you are my only refuge in affliction and bewilderment.

44

First of all, the above address is permanent for three months for which thank God. I have wandered all over Greece and now we have a wee very idyllic (almost *Strand Magazine*) home in the most beautiful island in the world and another long leave on account of my health (which is not in a very serious condition) my chief disease is a chronic lack of funds. So do answer me.

A. What about *Snaith?*

B. What about the "Don Juan" poems. Are any or all of them wanted for the *Review?*

C. What about the Article on Public Opinion? I can revise it if needed.

D. Please might I have the April and June numbers of the *Review* forwarded here. I have nothing to read at all. Also you promised that nice book of Norman Douglas! The numbers of the *Review* may have been sent to Smyrna, but there'll be no harm in sending another two copies here.

E. I am sending to London today the revised version of *Don Juan*, with alterations in the first two acts. (Sorry you hate the transcendental 3rd' one which I can't change much.) What shall I do with it when typed?

F. If you pass David Nutts you might turn in and ask them if my Italian Grammar is published. They refuse to write to me at all about it.

You know my poems are being reissued by Dent's with additions, including the "Ballad of Iskander." I forget if I wrote to the *Review* for formal permission. Would you see.

And now to God the Father. . . .

Come here and see us. It's a lovely place.

Ever yours,

H.* E. FLECKER.

* H. E. were the poet's official initials, Herman Elroy being his real name, He had adopted "James" when at Oxford, having a dislike for "Herman."

*June,* 1911.
*Casa Bogdanos,*
*Stratia,*
*Corfu.*

MY DEAR MAVRO:

Forgive a postcard; you shall have a letter very soon—but I have no writing paper left. A thousand thanks for your letter and for interviewing . . . . Mrs. ——. I have the proofs. I discover that she has added a whole damned appendix on Dante, cut my preface about and added to it. I have written to the reviser, Mr. T. Okey, who is presumably a scholar and a gentleman (You know him, I expect, he is a Dent-ist Danteite) expounding my sorrows to him . . . .——

The MS. of *Don Juan,* Acts 1 and 2, revised, is being sent straight away to you at the *E.R.* office; I expect it will be pretty correct, Miss Speakman (5 Duke Street, if you remember) being the best typist I have ever struck.

Persuade the Editor to take the long "Don Juan" poems for August. Frightfully obliged about the cheque; if not sent off already get Miss Francis to send it straight to the Capital & Counties Bank, Cambridge—as there is just a chance we may roll towards Italy in a week or so. This island is adorable but hot. I have started off on my new *Arabian Nights* play—it will be more marvellously unsaleable and unstageable than anything ever written.

I wish I could see you to thank you for all your kindness. It's so stupid of the *E. R.* to react: it won't *pay.* I must say I think its review columns, however, might be more authoritative on special subjects. But Benson, O my God! Tell the Editor that it spells net financial ruin.

Ever yours,
JAMES ELROY FLECKER.

*Casa Bogdanos Stratia,*
*Corfu,*
*Greece,*
*25th July.*

MY DEAR MAVRO:

Still here for three weeks more. Very well, and happy: but have achings after civilisation *de temps en temps.* Very sad not to have heard from you lately either in your capacity as Fairy Godmother or still better as Gossip of the literary world. For I feel direly severed from London. Also pending such far off time as that whenever my wife shall sell a house, or I receive a pension on the civil list pretty broke.

However, here's a poem for you which I think good and should like to know your opinion. If *E. R.* is really keen on having it and will promise to publish it this year it shall have it. If not, I have contracted the habit of sending my work to America.

Will you of your infinite and unremitting kindness tell me

(a) Whether a cheque is winging its way to my bank from the *E. R.*

(b) Whether the "Don Juan" poems are to appear, and when and which.

(c) Whether publication in America leaves one free to republish in England.

(d) Whether you received one copy of *Don Juan* play typed which I had sent to you.

Do forgive my so shamefully making use of you. Remember I am far from my own countree and you are the only person who has ever done a thing for me.

I have got the April No. of the *E. R.* in which I expect I see your hand: if you sent the book on *Capri* to Smyrna—I long to read it—I shall find it there on my return. I have written a joyous and Eastern poem which I have sent to America (I'll copy it out for you if

47

you send me a nice reply. It's 4 pages). I am bust on an *Arabian Nights* farce,\*, entirely popular, to run ten thousand nights (or at least 1001) ; love, intrigue, ghosts, pageants, everything in Arabian-English prose. My *Don Juan* I have sent to Trench again—it will never be played—not if I spend half a lifetime making it good.

Don't despair of the *E. R.*? A couple of villainous articles won't ruin the show.

How is the circulation? Tacebo. O Mavro why don't you and I edit it?

Peace upon thy head,

JAMES E. FLECKER.

P.S.—My new vol. of poems should be out soon : I am just sending off the proofs. Now my friend Frank Savery has written a not too flattering but well written article about me. Shall I get him to incorporate the new poems therein and send it to *E. R.*? He is a good writer.

*Casa Bogdanos,*
*Stratia,*
*Corfu, Greece,*
*28th July*, 1911.

Till 18th August.

Post 4—5 days.

MY DEAR MAVRO :

Here we are again !

After debating head in hand whether to send the enclosed

To America

To *English Review*,

To *Nash's Magazine*,

To *Nation*, cutting out the naughty verse about the humanist, I despatch it to you. *Fac quid vis* and nothing at all if it bores you. Curses on the fate that inspires me to write long poems !

---

\* The first conception of " Hassan."

I read to-day with delight that Sir Percy Bunting * is dead. I hope he had a nasty " râle," and is now being whipped round heaven by a lot of shamelessly naked Cherubim.

Thine,
JAMES ELROY FLECKER.

*Casa Bogdanos,*
*Stratia,*
*Corfu,*
*August* 11.

Forgot to mention. A lady has published an *Artist in Corfu.* Could you get hold of it and send it to me and I'll review it in a few lines. This is base deceit. I want the book and can't afford him (18s. absurd !). Still a few lines of criticism from the man on the spot might be welcome. Will pay postage. Have got July *English Review,* but not April No. for which I yearn. Ghost story is rather freely horrid. Am on half pay which is damnable ; so if could have " Don Juan " poems in August we would be very glad. Should like to see proof. After all Mrs. —— (a very nice woman and a friend of mine) has been in twice in 5 months. Rather like Robertson M.P. but piqued at his taking Watson seriously. Wrote to tell him so. Am sending many things to America in hope of raising money.

Thine,
J. E. F.

*Corfu,*
*August* 1911.

MY DEAR MAVRO :
Blessings on your head for your letter. Please don't worry about that article on public opinion—it's been to *T. P.'s* already. The novel is packed at Smyrna whither

---

* A once well-known authority on public morals.

we return on the 20th. So please write British Consulate, Smyrna, where letters will await me, and come and see us when you come to Athens—it's so near. You won't be quarantined if you come *viâ* Brindiso. As for *Don Juan*, Trench writes he has resigned : F. Harrison of Haymarket has one copy. I had nothing from Granville Barker : merely a word of refusal from Little Theatre. Horniman ? Could you send it to that great lady ? Thine,

J. E. FLECKER.

I have got your letter and proof. Let me know what you think of my corrections—I send them by this post. To fight —— who killed the Savoy and murdered John Davidson, two methods

(1) Get a declaration from them that the *E. R.* is immoral and take a libel action. This should have been done re *Spectator*.

(2) Get Cunningham Graham and go round and *birch* the Junior Partner. He will be ashamed to take action for being birched. If you don't fight you're doomed.

Just another word to fill the P.C. up entirely. If the proofs don't come let me know at once. I can catch the letter at 40 rue Scoufa, Athens. Other letters to Smyrna. A thousand apologies for packed postcard.

*Athens,*
*August* 1911.

Have just got a letter from you and a postcard from Jack. Am off to Beyrut (British Consulate) on Wednesday, *viâ* Alexandria. Do send me a line and make that pig Jack write. Wish the devil I could come to Munich with my lady wife : still we have a great time. Am as fit as a fiddle : hope it will last. Am on a new play—1st act finished called *Hassan of Bagdad*—a marvel ! All my copies of *Don Juan* are with Managers. Have written many poems. Why *don't* you send things to the

A Watering-place on the Lebanon.

The Favourite Printed Hangings.

[To face p. 50.

*English Review*, stupid (11, Henrietta St., W.C.).   Joy
to both of you.   I do a Waring ?   In Vishnuland what
avatar ?

JAMES.

*The British Consulate-General,*
*Beirut, Syria,*
23/10/11.

MY DEAR MAVRO :

Ages and ages ! and I at Beirut.   It's a long way
away.   A filthy town, pleasant country, camels, palms,
missionaries, and traces of the O.B. psalm.

O, most excellent and perfect, I would write to you of
business—this literary business whereby I, by great
slaving, acquire between ten and fifteen pounds a year.

A. Re *Don Juan* O, Mavro, it will never be played.   I
have not heard from the gent you sent it to, though I
wrote.

B. Act 1 of my new play *Hassan of Bagdad* is with
George Alexander who has acknowledged receipt thereof.
I asked him to return it to you when he was tired of it.
I am really shameless, but I promise you, you will like
reading it.

C. You have a copy of my ballad "Bryan of Brittany"
(How does one spell it ?)   Would you ask the *E. R.* if
they want it.

I mentioned to 'em without being offensive, that I
thought four pound was a little cheap for three crowded
pages of verse.   Hope they weren't annoyed.

Haven't had my October No. yet.   Want it bad.
Did you get my " Golden Journey " to " Samarkand "
dialogue poem ?   That's for the *E. R.* too.

D. Please tell Martin Secker if you see him that I
have not forgotten about my novel : but that after the
first two chapters it wants almost entire rewriting.
Nevertheless he shall have it by the beginning of
January.

51

Never got your friend's book about Capri; would so much like it. Nor did my efforts obtain a copy of Miss Atkinson on Corfu, to review.

This is a horrid selfish letter and I'll end it. Joy be with you.

JAMES ELROY FLECKER.

*OΛA XPEIAZONTAI*, as a Gk. innkeeper said to my wife when she asked that a jerry might be supplied in the bedroom.

*The British Consulate-General,*
*Beirut, Syria,*
*December 10th, 1911.*

*To* MR HAROLD MONRO
SIR,

I experience some difficulty in writing to you as I do not know whether you know of me or not. I have contributed poetry to the *Nation* and *English Review* regularly; and Messrs. Dent's are just reissuing my volume " 36 " poems. I should of course be very pleased if you could give me a month in the *Poetry Review*, and had I been in London I should doubtless have arranged to see you about the matter. As it is I confess I am frightened of being snubbed, for of course I am not used to having MSS. rejected, as I have now among however small a circle an established reputation.

I am sorry to have to adopt this offensive, egoistic attitude : when there is no one to perform the office of introduction, one must do it oneself.

I am sending you by the same post a poem " Bryan of Brittany," unpublished ; I presume that if you publish unpublished poems you would pay for them at *English Review* rates. The poem has not been shown to any Editor before, and is I think, one of my best ; if you reject it I hope it will appear in the *English Review*, but as they have one of mine in hand at present I am afraid it would not come out for some months.

52

If you want shorter poems, or poems already published of course I should be only too delighted to send them.

Whether I should join the Society I do not know. Is it for poets or for critics? Or for both? Please send me its prospectus.

I am, Sir,
Yours faithfully,
JAMES ELROY FLECKER.

*The British Consulate-General,*
*Beirut, Syria,*
*December* 10, 1911.

MY DEAR MAVRO:

I shall begin to think I have committed some sin against you. Why this long silence? My postcard sent to Brindisi came back the other day; but the *E. R.* tells me you are still there; working hard.

I live here in clear sunshine among damned fools, very happy however, when I can get out of town a bit, and wander in the Lebanon. Both of us are a bit sick of Beirut, but it might be much worse: and soon we hope to spend a golden holiday at Damascus and Baalbek.

Fontana, Consul at Aleppo passed through yesterday. A subscriber to the *E. R.* and in every way a delight to exiles. However, am really happy except that have not arranged yet for anything to do when in about 2 years' time we chuck up the service. On leave next year I hope to work it.

I have just written to the Editor of *Poetry Review* enclosing " Bryan of Brittany " (3 jolly new verses added), asking him for a month. I surely deserve it, but I don't know him or what clique he belongs to. If you know him say a good word for me. I sent " B. of B." having nothing else save a jolly little poem I sent to the *Nation*, unpublished at present. The *E. R.* has my " Samarkand " poem: I hope it's to come out. I have all my *E. R.'s* now ; Oct., Nov., Dec. Many thanks to Manager. Think I can get a subscriber here.

" Ever " by Walter de la Mare is delightful.

Do write to me and tell me how the world is moving. I get so few letters from England.

Ever yours,

J. E. FLECKER.

*Xmas day.*

*Carissimo Franco :*

We are weekending at Damascus, but our address is British Consulate, Beirut, as usual. Do write : do I owe you a letter ? I know I would like one from you. Busy rewriting my accursed novel.

This town is interesting, but I wish we were at Chipping Candover all the same.

Thine ever,

JAMES.

# REMINISCENCES 1912

JANUARY was very rainy, but what with social duties, some dances and amateur theatricals, the time passed quickly. My husband was then working at *Hassan* and writing the *Gates of Damascus*, sitting at a large table covered with one of his Persian printed cloths ; under this table we had placed an oil-stove which, when it condescended not to smell, was a real comfort in the wet season—no other heating apparatus being available and the sitting-room having a chilly floor of black and white marble flags. Then one morning we awoke to find Beyrut was being shelled by the Italians. Three destroyers were to be seen outside the harbour. shelling two wretched Turkish gunboats, whose officers all slept quietly in their respective houses in town, so that only a few distracted sailors were sunk together with the old craft. Some shells burst suddenly on the quays, killing a number of gaping Arabs. Then more shells shot over the town, causing a general panic. The hotels flew their whole collection of foreign flags, while the consular body in uniform were rushing about in frenzied excitement. J. E. Flecker has related his experiences of that day in a spirited article " Forgotten Warfare," which he sent to the *New Statesman* in the autumn of 1914, and which now is to be found in *Collected Prose*.

That Italian attack marked the end of our happy days at Beyrut. Shortly after an incident occurred which was greatly to disturb our quietude. We were sharing the annexe of the hotel where we stayed with a Russian couple, the Russian military attaché and his wife, both no longer young. Soon the lady showed signs of wishing to monopolise the use of the common hall that separated our two apartments. A line of screens was erected that threatened to cut us off from our front sitting-room by leaving an increasingly narrow passage along the wall. One day issuing from the bedroom after the noonday siesta my husband found the way practically blocked by the expanding screens. He then did what every spirited person would have done; he gave a violent kick to the nearest screen which toppled over on to its neighbours, so that three inanimate screens lay on the floor and a very animate lady appeared at the opposite bedroom door.

The scene was soon enlivened by the hotel manager, who was a German and not particularly amiable and by the husband as usual very full of beer. I had at first succeeded in persuading my husband to let me tackle the situation, which was a delicate one, and had pushed him back into the bedroom, but when he heard the bellowing voice of the husband climbing the stairs he came out, to my great annoyance, to face the opponent with the clear conscience of one who is in the right. The colleague was noisy and disagreeable and his wife was the picture of injured and indignant virtue. The consequence was we ceased being on speaking terms with the couple, and the lady always being about the place made things awkward, we two belonging to the thin-skinned and our persecutors to the tough-skinned variety of humans. In a very few days my husband became so worried we decided to leave the hotel and go to an English pension where we found two nice rooms. But the spell was broken and a series of unfortunate circumstances followed. The food was intolerable at our new residence, the mosquitoes more aggressive, the street-dogs fought like demons at night below our windows, and when we had driven these away by volleys of missiles, such as medicine bottles, or water, usually followed by the glass or jug, then from a neighbouring

H. F. AT THE SAME DATE. TAKEN BY J. E. F.

BEYROUT: J. E. F. IN 1912, TAKEN BY H. F.

[To face p. 56.

garden-pond the chorus of frogs broke out and prevented all rest. We decided we would go as soon as possible to our summer quarters in some village of the Lebanon, and my husband began searching for a tiny house to let. As soon as this was found at Areya I was taken with a slow fever and could scarcely crawl about when in May we moved to the " small house with arches three " in the midst of a large garden containing several other cottages.

There was a fine view over the valleys and mountains from the balcony beneath the three arches, the jasmine shading the entrance to the garden side was in full bloom ; as for the pomegranate trees there were several, splashing their bright scarlet touch all over the grounds. But here we were not the only tenants, and we could not, as at Corfu, enjoy sitting outside the house. Some of the neighbours were noisy or quarrelsome, though the land-lord who lived in one of his tiny houses not far off was a very discreet and polite person, besides being one of the most industrious and clever men I have met in the East. He belonged to the ant-like species. A bachelor of indefinable age, rather tall, very thin with reddish hair, a short beard and greenish eyes, he was up at daybreak and never stopped working until late at night ; a clever carpenter and builder he was either repairing or adding to his numerous erections, painting, arranging a water-pipe here, digging a cistern there.

On Sundays he put on a black threadbare frock-coat over a white shirt and was to be met going to church with our Greek cook, Angela, who, though on weekdays she was always grumbling at him calling him an old miser, was very proud to go to mass in the company of " Moussiou Missel," as she called him, who belonged to the Orthodox Syrian Community and was a very devout Christian. One Sunday Angela and he decided that an old family icon of the virgin, a tenth century painting of the Cretan school which I had, must be taken to mass and be incensed by the priest. It was wrapped in a silk scarf and reverently carried by Monsieur Michel a four miles walk to the nearest village possessing an Orthodox chapel. The dark colours on a gold ground of the icon and its ancient appearance created a sensation among the simple village folk, who whispered it might be one of the miraculous virgins painted by St. Luke and Angela was very much impressed.

This creature, a native of the island of Andros, had a fiendish temper, but was rather a good cook and, having served some time at the house of the British Consul General, had some notions of English ways and cooking. Her favourite dish was Irish stew, which she had Hellenized into " Ariston." A good worker, she had nerves and probably some Arab blood in her veins. She did not get on with my husband, whom she bullied, and they screamed at each other without either understanding what the other said, so that when I was taken seriously ill and nearly died in the night the situation was critical. It chanced that the young officer with whom we had spent Christmas at Damascus turned up the very next day. Seeing my husband in trouble, with a very ill-tempered servant as only help, he mentioned that a Danish lady belonging to a mission somewhere in the desert, east of Damascus, had arrived at the village where he was staying with his wife and new-born son, on a holiday, and that she would no doubt come and nurse me if she were asked. My husband immediately wrote to her. Next day she was there, and I shall never forget what I owe her.

Besides being an excellent nurse, this lady was cultured and very entertaining ; she used during meals to tell my husband many good stories of the very primitive nomadic tribes the Danish mission dealt with. Among other amusing incidents of her life with the Arabs, I remember she told how, shortly after her arrival at the mission, she had had the visit of a sheik who came to tell her confidentially that her hair, which was turning grey, was a matter of scandal, that his people could not understand how a woman of her standing could be so indecent, and that if she wished to remain among them she must have it dyed with henna, as all their elderly people do, the men as well as the women. She had had to keep up a perpetual fight against this incongruous pretention, and for the first two years had been more or less tabooed by the most conservative elements of the various tribes. My husband was much amused to hear that another lady who had belonged to the same mission had been so upset by the general reproach of immorality addressed to her grey chignon that she succumbed and appeared one day crowned with a flaming red mass of henna-dyed hair.

My husband was then preparing a Turkish examination and did not have much time for literary work. The heat was very trying in July and August and the journey down and up at the hottest hour of the day, there being only one afternoon train that left Beyrut at 2 p.m., reaching Areya at 4, was very exhausting. On the whole, my husband bore the heat very well, what he again missed was the lack of intelligent society. One day T. E. Lawrence turned up early in the morning. As we enquired how he had got to Areya, there being no train at that hour, he quietly explained that he had arrived by the night train, but not wishing to disturb us had slept on the floor in the station to the scandal of the station-master. My husband was delighted to be able to talk literature and Oxford again, and to hear of the " amazing boy's " astonishing adventures in Asia Minor. The photo given in frontispiece of J. E. F. in Arabic dress was taken by Lawrence on the three-arched balcony, and that of the " amazing boy," as Roy sometimes spoke of him, by my husband.

Another day the young officer from Damascus came to ask us to go with them to the cedars high up on one

of the peaks where a group of them still stand. I was
kept lying in bed, but my husband went, greatly enjoying
the trip. Then we had an exciting time with the Druses
fighting the Maronites in our neighbourhood. In
September I was at last allowed to get up and we could
again go for short walks or drives, but the heat was still
great, and we both felt run down. My husband wrote
to ask for a two months' leave to have a change after
his exam. which, unfortunately, we heard some weeks
later, he did not pass successfully—which added to his
general discontent. On November 5th, his twenty-
eighth birthday, we had a delightful lunch in the garden.
Angela had secured a wild duck, which she prepared in
the Greek way with green olives and tomatoes. The
jasmine and roses were still in bloom and the prospect
of soon greeting again severer skies and the mists and
dark of an English winter made my husband enjoy very
keenly the cloudless beauty of that autumn day.

Early in December we said good-bye to Areya, and,
driving straight down to Beyrut harbour, we took our
passage on a Khedivial Line steamer for Alexandria,
there to catch a P. & O. cargo to Marseilles. Our boat
crawled down in view of the Syrian coast. At Jaffa we
went ashore and had a good lunch on a terrace overlooking the new extensive orange plantations and
wondered at the innumerable camels that thronged the
town and were crouching all round the harbour quays.
In the orange gardens that surround the town the autumn
trees were in blossom and their fragrance fought successfully the terrible camel stench. Our captain, who never
seemed to go ashore, was a pessimistic and spleenful
Englishman who had never been home for years and
seemed to have no tie with any part of the world, not
even with his ship, for he said he was so tired of the
monotonous trip performed twice in the month along
the dull coasts of Egypt and Syria. He was an elderly
man who had had command in the Indian Ocean, but

THE LEBANON :
BEDAWI CAMEL-DRIVERS.

A SMALL HOTEL ON
THE LEBANON.

THE HEAD OF A CARAVAN ON THE ROAD FROM DAMASCUS
LED BY A SMALL DONKEY.

TAIL OF CARAVAN

[*To face p.* 60.

now, for who knows what reason, had to be content with this not very interesting job. Most of the crew were Greeks, as well as the chief engineer, a perpetually smiling jocose person who had a wife in Alexandria preparing cakes and tasty dishes for his return. The Greek stewards having heard at Port Said that the Greek Army had taken Salonica from the Turks, all came rushing to me with the news in great excitement, while the chief engineer, whose patriotic ardour revived, confessed to me that he was sorry his wife at Alexandria had prevented him by her tears and entreaties from volunteering for the Greek fleet.

On arriving at Alexandria we passed before the P. & O. and saw it was preparing to leave. We just had time to scramble on board with our fifteen bags and parcels. Among these was a basket with two unfortunate chameleons that had now begun to look very shabby, and were never to turn a bright hue again. Our ship came from China and its passengers were a strange lot of worn-out creatures who had most of them not returned for years, some for a whole lifetime, and had by now been on board over two months. My husband was irritated with them because when we passed Corsica they called it Sicily, and none of them left the boat at Marseilles to reach England sooner, but passively faced another weary week on board, though they were thoroughly tired of the boat and the monotonous food.

We found splendid cold weather at Marseilles, and my husband decided we would go to Arles for a day or two and see it on the way. It was freezing hard when we arrived there late in the day. The Hotel du Forum, in spite of the " calorifère " of which it boasted, was deadly cold. Fortunately there was an old world fireplace in the room, and we soon had a blazing wood fire to cheer us up.

The basket with the chameleons was placed before it, but, alas, only the smaller of the two seemed to have a

61

spark of life left in its body. The other looked pathetic amongst its orange leaves; its head, with the large globular eyes deeply sunk in their sockets, had taken on the expression of a blind old man's wrinkled face. Not knowing what the attitude of a chameleon is in winter we thought it might be in lethargy, and did not like to throw it in the fire. The smaller one was to reach Paris in a semi-conscious state, was placed on a twig and found hanging by its tail dead in the morning.

Next day on waking we found Arles swept by a bitter north blast and looking very stiff and skeleton-white like a city of the moon. A bright sun was shining, and we wandered round looking at the delightful cloister of St. Trophime and stopping before the head of Cæsar as a boy, in the museum opposite. We also went to see the artist who had decorated with Provençal subjects the dining-room of the Forum. He was a very simple and nice person, and showed us a number of his Arlesian pictures and his wife in the picturesque costume of the place which since the war is no longer worn at Arles, except by a few very old women. In his company, and that of his pretty daughter Mireille, we drove to the beautiful ruined citadel of Les Baux, whose sixteenth century fortified mansions had been razed by Cardinal Richelieu. Their mutilated remains perched high upon a rocky hill show a finely decorated stone window here, a gabled doorway further on, framing the blue sky and the elegant line of the plain towards Avignon. My husband liked the sparse intellectual landscape that reminds one of a toned down Greece.

We stayed some days with my mother at Neuilly, and then he left for England where I joined him a week later. We first went to Oxford, which my husband wished to show me. We went round his old rooms at Trinity and stayed at the same furnished apartments where he had often stayed as a bachelor and where the landlady was an excellent cook. I shall never forget the

impression of quietude and restful peace we felt at
Oxford ; its misty grey sky and the stately order of its
old colleges were in such pleasing contrast with the
cruel light and disorderly picturesque of the East.
Flecker was delighted to be there again, and was in very
high spirits. We went to stay with his parents at
Cheltenham for a few days, and then returned to London.
He hoped to find a job in England, but he was not
feeling very strong again, and the doctors he saw, both
in England and in Paris, advised him to go back to the
sunnier clime of Syria. We left for Paris on Christmas
Eve. I remember it was a frosty sunny day, and the sea
was a pale blue and calm as the sky. But our hearts
were heavy. In Paris we spent a merry Christmas and
New Year. Mr. Jack Beazley was over at the time, and
my husband was glad to see him again and to live once
more in his company the old life of a student in the
Latin quarter, and in the then still existing Café Vachette.

---

*British Consulate-General,*
*Beirut.*

10 Jan. [1912.]

My Dear and Antient Franco :

This to tell you that I have written to Messrs. Dent
telling them to send you a copy of my *Forty-Two Poems*,
which *comme son nom l'indique*, simply means the old 36
and 6 new ones. However for the little interest it has,
take it.

I am plodding along slowly rewriting *The King of
Alsander*. Nothing in God's earth can infuse any reality
into the tale ; so I confine myself to polishing, and
writing it up less heavily, and hope it may be a popular
success—'tis all it's good for.

We have two months winter here and are now under-
going them—just rain five days out of six, and the 6th
day very blue—like to-day. Beirut's a hole to live in,
but a fine place to get out of—the Lebanon, Baalbek,

Damascus. I would give anything to cross the desert to Palmyra, but can't get leave enough. Not that Palmyra is much in itself. Colonnades of fine pillars with horrid little brackets, it appears, where the bourgeois donor placed his edifying bust. But the desert it appears, is wonderful, and does not entirely consist of miles and miles and miles of sand.

Well, the East is a bit of a refuge from those interminable old Greeks, and judging from my latest efforts I shall go down to fame (if I go) as a sort of Near East Kipling. Modern Greece and modern Greek folk songs are very good things too—a very strange bridge between East and West.

Meantime, O Franko, I long much—we both of us long, for civilised company. It has been supplied to us so far by one Lawrence demy of Magdalen—a strange boy who tramps Syria on foot and digs Hittites for Hogarth, and F——, our Consul at Aleppo, a glorious specimen of high worn out æsthetic Genoese aristocracy. As for Lawrence and his Hittites 'tis a moot point whether the svastika seal wherewith I am sealing this is Hittite or not ; I intend to ask Hogarth when he comes through here in April. I am acting Vice-Consul here for three more months at least.

I expect and hope to take leave before the end of the year. We shall come back may be through Europe and visit one Franco on the way. It is time you were visible again ! When in England I am going to look about seriously for a decent post (perhaps as lecturer in English Literature, perhaps on a paper) as I have not the slightest intention of spending more than another two years in the service. All the same it's an odd life and good for the soul.

Farewell : and I pray you write. If you send the Essay on my Poems renewed to date to the *English Review* (new address Country Life Buildings, 20 Tavistock Street, Covent Garden) they might very likely take it

T. E. LAWRENCE

AND HIS SERVANT IN
THE GARDEN,
AREYA.

[*To face p.* 64.

and it would be good both for you and me. And why
O why did you never send them a story, insensate?
Answer me!

Ever your old friend.

JAMES.

P.S.—Marry.

*British Consulate-General,*
*Beirut.*

*5 June,* 1912.

MY DEAR MAVRO:

Rescue me from financial despair I pray of you and
get the *E. R.* to print my " Journey to Samarkand."

There is an exquisite poem rejected by the *Nation*—
perhaps the *E. R.* would like it. There is the ballad of
" Bryan of Brittany " unpublished—and what the use
is of going on scratching when one can't get one's best
work published I don't know.

Am in a black fury with the art of the pen. Finances
rotten : and damned Americans wrote and asked me for
stuff and I sent them my best and they sent it all back
again. As for that sow the high bourgeois public it
seems a poem must be crude long and preachifying to
tickle it.

Hush Mavro! Don't let 'em know—but I hate *all*
of them—all what you call the grey social tinges—
Galsworthy, Masefield's new ventures, Granville Barker's, even Arnold Bennett (why was that damned
vulgar potboiler *The Card* praised in the *E. R.*). Don't
tell me you praised it, Mavro, or I'll call you out. And
why was such insufficient praise given to that noble work
*Zuleika Dobson?*

Forgive my ill temper. My wife just as we had got an
idyllic house on the Lebanon caught a slow fever from
which she is just recovering. Except Hogarth and his
two fellow archæologists intermittently resplendent on
the way to or from Carckemish we never see a civilised

soul. I know all about the Lebanon. Hope to get to England for ever next year—between you and me. Will accept editorship of *E. R.* (you being transferred to *Little Folks*) or any post above £400 a year. Do write to me—it is a cheerful and joyous thing to get a letter in these climes.

Thank Editor for cheque for review of Corfu book. I made a mistake in correcting a mistake of course. The woman's Babadoni is not Papa, but Barba Antoni.

Now do write,

Ever yours,

JAMES ELROY FLECKER.

P.S.—Please tell them I have not got May No. of *English Review* and should particularly like to have it.

British Consulate-General,

Beirut.

11 July, 1912.

MY DEAR MAVRO :

Glad you're going to publish " Santorin " : have immediately written to *Poetry Review* to withdraw it. I sent it them because I thought the *English Review* would publish my *poem* " The Golden Journey to Samarkand " (the one that began with the Divan of the West and had the Jews in). Now *where* is that poem? Does the *E. R.* want it ? If it does not want it please send it round to Mr. Monro of *Poetry Review*, but of course I'd infinitely rather the *E. R.* had it, but the *E. R.* has now had it for six months without saying a word about it. I am somewhat in despair. Can't it be printed with " Santorin " ? If it is lost I can send another.

I was extremely grateful to you for sending me the poems of De la Mare. I have enjoyed them greatly : he is a good artist in his limits : it is a pity he has set them so narrow. The poem on Arabia is admirable and for devilishly clever simplicity the epitaph on the *Lady of*

66

WASHING-DAY IN THE GARDEN AT AREYA.

A FAMILY GROUP OF DRUSES.

[To face p. 66.

the *West Country* is marvellous. There is much Housman, and as my wife says much Poe : but the gruesome ones are the best. He might sow his "silver may" a bit thinner. Is he personally as charming as his poems? Do you want a review of him by the way? I expect you have already done it yourself.

Ever yours,<br>JAMES ELROY FLECKER.

P.S.—The second act of the *Golden Journey to Samarkand* is not finished. The 1st act is ample for anyone to judge of.

I sent the *Smart Set*, the 1st act, which by a clever cut can be made a complete little drama ending with the fall of Hassan. Would the *E. R.* like it? If so I'll get them to send it round to you.

*British Consulate-General,*<br>
*Beirut,*<br>
26 *July*, 1912.

MY DEAREST FRANCO :

What's the good of writing letters? We have too much to talk about. Whatever may be my slackness in writing be assured I shall leave no stone unturned to come and see you when I come on leave. Am not yet sure if I shall take leave this year. My wife must go and see her mother, so I probably shall go with her, for to tell the truth I don't look forward even to a temporary spell of celibacy : even Oxford would bore me, alone.

Unfortunately my wife caught a damned Mediterranean low fever which lasted 2 months : it is gone now. Summer on the Lebanon in such a charming place as we are is Arcadia : though the place is not so madly beautiful as Corfu by any means. I come to Beirut 3 times a week only : the other days I dream under pine trees, or bang the piano. I'm not a Neville Forbes but I can play better than the old Nort—I had to learn to accompany Hellé's violin—and at times I write a poem or revise the poor old *King of Alsander*, whom I hope to send to the publisher in a week from now, I can't do much with him.

The August *English Review* will contain a poem of mine, " Santorin." I hate the East—the Lebanon is Christian thank God—but I have written (does the old James speak ?) the best Eastern poems in the language.

When I send my novel I will ask the Publisher to send a proof direct to you and if you care to help me revise the same, I shall be very grateful.

I talked to Hogarth who was here about trying to get a job at Oxford. Shall have had enough of this job by this time next year. But where shall I get £350 a year in England. I won't live on less.

Ever your affectionate,<br>JAMES.

Am reading *Innocence of Father Brown* by Chesterton. It is simply adorable. But he won't convert me. If you haven't read it you get it in *Tauchnitz*, No. 4282. Write.

[*To* EDWARD MARSH]

British Consulate General,<br>Beyrut,<br>Syria,<br>Oct. 12th, 1912.

DEAR SIR :

Many thanks for your offer to include me in your anthology. I shall be of course very glad to appear in the company of my old friend Rupert Brooke. If you just ask Messrs. Dent yourself anything and say I have consented or shew them this letter, I am sure they will consent. I expect only stipulating for a notice to say which book they are from.

As for the poems which you have chosen to represent me, I am myself, if you will forgive me, against " Joseph and Mary." I would rather you took one or two shorter

FORTRESS OF DJEBEIL.

THE PORT OF DJEBEIL (THE ANCIENT BYBLOS).

[*To face p.* 68.

poems, and would be kind enough to choose from these :

> " Rioupéroux,"
> " Tenebris interlucentem,"
> " The Saracens " (or " Pillage "),

or if you care for the less lyrical style, the " Ballad of Hampstead Heath." But you have my leave to take anything you like, and welcome.

Will you think it impertinent if I make one or two suggestions?

One is that your anthology be the first to include, if it does not include already, the " Pirate Ship " of Richard Middleton (page 37 of his poems, Fisher Unwin) which is a masterpiece. I never knew poor Middleton who was murdered by the British Public, but his suicide this year was one of the tragedies of Literature. I hope you have chosen De la Mare's " Arabia."

Letters of this sort are apt to get prolix : but I hope to be in London in December when perhaps I may have the pleasure of meeting you.

I subscribe to the dedication to Robert Bridges cordially. But I shall dedicate my next book to the memory of Richard Middleton.

Yours faithfully,
(H.) J. E. FLECKER.

*Beyrut,*

*Oct. 30th,* 1912.

MY DEAR MAVRO :

I leave this cursed place the 10th November and my address till Nov. 28 is

> chez Madame Skiadaressi
> 10 rue du Marché
> Neuilly Seine
> Paris.

whither please send proofs of " Gates of Damascus."

69

Hope to see you about 1st Dec. I am singing pæans to the victorious all day long.

JAMES E. FLECKER.
*[December, 1912.]*

*Chez Madame Skiadaressi*
10 *rue du Marché*
*Neuilly Seine*
*Paris.*
21 *Nov.*

MY DEAR MAVRO :
I shall be coming to England, alone, and for the serious purpose of finding a livelihood less abominable than the Oriental Career, on Wednesday next. My chief and first object will be to see the only person who seems to take an interest in this unfortunate poet—viz. yourself—and reward you for all your kindness by being a bore. Where and how can I see you on Thursday morning (28th)—if indeed you are not afraid of my still barbarous Turkish manners? Please send me a line to above address by return.

Ever yours,
JAMES E. FLECKER.

*Dean Close School,*
*Cheltenham.*
*[December, 1912.]*

DEAR MARSH :
The above is my address. I should much appreciate a copy of " Georgian Verse " if you would send me one.

I stupidly left some dull papers (the " Outcry " or something working-mannish and a Report) in the waiting-room at the Admiralty. If they happen to be encumbering the place I should be grateful if you would forward them to me. But they are of no importance ; please don't look for them.

I am having the 2nd act of my play typed and shall

send the 1st 2 acts to you in the course of the week with a synopsis of the third. Please do not be bothered with them, but perhaps if you yourself think they are worth bothering Barker about, you might do so.

One more abuse of your kindness. I think I must get a rotten little appointment at once. You told me the Cambridge Appointments Board was good. But I don't know Benson. Do you think it would be worth while sending my application through you for you to forward to Benson?

Yours very sincerely,

J. E. FLECKER.

*Brown's Hotel,*

3, *Craven Street,*

*Charing Cross.*

*Thursday.*

Thanks for your letter. I will try and come round to-morrow evening at 11. If I don't reach you by 11.30 don't expect me!

Yours,

H. E. FLECKER.

P.S.—Shall be in Oxford Sunday.

E. MARSH, ESQ.,
> The Admiralty,
>> London, S.W.

170, *Walton Street,*

*Oxford.*

DEAR MARSH :

The above is my right address. I may have given you 150 by mistake. We shall be in at 6 o'clock and hope to see you!

H. E. FLECKER.

E. MARSH, ESQ.,
> All Soul's College,
>> Oxford.

71

12, *Dorset Square*,
*N.W.*
[*December*, 1912.]

DEAR MARSH :

Many thanks for your kind invitation. I'll be round at 1.45 at the Golden Ship with my dramatic works under my arm.

Yours sincerely,
J. E. FLECKER.

12, *Dorset Square*,
*N.W.*
*Tuesday* (*December*, 1912).

MY DEAR MARSH :

I enclose the play : Acts I and II and synopsis of III.

I hadn't time to go and see Rupert this afternoon, alas.

I've got fixed up to review your book from the *E. Review*.

Yours gratefully and sincerely,
J. E. FLECKER.

12, *Dorset Square*,
*N.W.*
[*December*, 1912.]

With many apologies for abominably unbusiness-like behaviour.

Please send the MS. of Act II back to me at this address. I enclose an envelope for him. Don't trouble to register.

Am sending MS. separate
envelope by same mail.

> *Chez Madame Skiadaressi,*
> 10, *rue du Marché,*
> *Neuilly Seine,*
> *Paris,*
> 27*th Dec.* [1912.]

MY DEAR MONRO :

Thanks for your letter. First, about my poems. Most of what Rupert saw has either been or is going to be published. What I want you to publish is the Prologue and Epilogue to the " Golden Journey to Samarkand." I don't know if I showed it you—but it's no good saying you don't like it because every one says it's the best poem I (or perhaps anyone else—I borrow this hearty egoism from old John Davidson—it's a shame that it should be the only mannerism that still pays) has ever written. The epilogue was written as a poem in itself but I shall turn it into the final scene of my Eastern play of which Marsh now has the first 2 acts.

I think you kept dark the name of the gentleman who was so lukewarm in my praise in the *Poetry Review*. grrr.

You must not write in favour of the Turks ; you may write against the Bulgars if you like ; but you should know that every mosque in Stamboul was built by Christians and everything of any beauty in the town is Christian. The Eastern Christian is a wonderful fellow and it is he who is fighting the Turk, who can't write a poem, or sing a song, or drive a train.

As for John Davidson please send to Paris at once (so that I can write before I leave) just the 3 or 4 little volumes (*Fleet Street Eclogues, New Ballads,* etc.), which won't cost much to send—a few pence. You will get them back. I am remember a Consul and a business man. (I ought to ask you how much money I am going to rake in, but I won't.)

I tried hard to find some honourable job in London till September, but as I *won't* be usher at a preparatory

73

school in Yorkshire I must go back to the East a while. It's rotten and miserable but I shall have heaps of time to write. If anybody wants to give me a few hundred pounds send me a wire and I'll come !

Ever yours,
J. E. FLECKER.

## A SONG FROM THE LEBANON

When viewless roses
In bright winds linger
When rose-soft anthems
    In light-winds play
My fragrant love
Will bring me the spring time,
Sailing to Lebanon
    Over the bay.

Vainly I sought
In Beyrut valley
Those red and blue flowers
    That bloomed so gay,
The olives rustled
And bowed and whispered
Hyacinths, hyacinths
    Wait for the day.

Wait for the girl who
Sat in our shadow
With the sea in her eyes
    And her breast as the spray,
Then we will order
All red and blue flowers
To break into blossom
    And sing on her way.

Sing, red and blue flowers,
Sing gentle olives,
Rose-laden South Wind
    Sing you and say

That fragrant girl
Has brought us the Spring time
Sailing to Lebanon
Over the bay.

J. E. F., *Feb.* 13.

About the middle of January my husband had to
return to Beyrut. I was not very strong and the doctor
advised me to stay in a colder climate for another two
months so as to get rid of the Malta fever germ which
I was supposed to have caught on the Lebanon. So
we decided he would go alone and that I would follow
in March. He left feeling very depressed and on the
next morning he was back at Neuilly. He had got off
the Marseilles train at the first stop, Laroche, had spent
the night there and taken the first train back to Paris,
having decided he could very well leave by the next
boat a week later. I can never remember without a
pang that return from Laroche and his second departure
a week later, when I very nearly left with him and only
stayed back fearing I might be a nuisance instead of a
comfort if I had a relapse of that horrid fever. But I
was full of fears and saw him off with a sinking heart
while he this time was in very good spirits. The steamer
he took reached Syria by way of Constantinople, and it
was on that trip passing Rhodes that he saw the small
island of Hyali and wrote the poem bearing its name, as
also " A Ship an Isle a sickle Moon." He reached
Beyrut early in February and looked round for a house.
He found one belonging to a professor of the American
college who was going on leave, but just as he was
arranging it he caught a chill and fell seriously ill. I
had set out in March to join him and when we got to
Alexandria the Messageries agent handed me a letter
in which my husband said he had been sent to hospital
by the doctor but was already better. He gave no details
and I shall never forget the anxious hours I spent on

that boat in Alexandria harbour fearing the worst and having to wait a whole day and night before we started again. And then I was told we should have a five days' quarantine, some cholera cases having occurred in Egypt and that I should not be allowed to land at Beyrut but would have to be taken up to Tripoli and back. I imagined Roy's disappointment when he was so impatiently waiting for me to arrive.

When we reached Beyrut, I saw my husband in Cook's boat being rowed up to the *Lotus*. He was allowed to come on board and spend the quarantine with me. He was in high spirits at having been able to join me but was not well and I was very anxious. When at last we landed at Beyrut and reached the little house he had rented he had to lie down most of the day. Soon the heat became unbearable in that one-floored house and the doctor advised me to take him up on the Lebanon to Brumana, where there was a decent hotel. On the terrace of that hotel where beautiful pink acacias were in full bloom he wrote some of his finest poems, " Brumana," " Taoping," and the two translations, " Pannyra," and " The Gate of the Armies." He also finished "In Hospital" and " Hyali," and wrote the lively preface to his new volume of poems, " The Golden Journey to Samarkand." But he was getting no better and I was growing more anxious every day seeing the climate was not bracing enough and that there was no time to lose. I insisted on knowing what the doctor thought best. He at last said that it would probably be a good thing to take my husband to Leysin. We managed somehow to get away and on May 19th took the first boat we could find, which was an Italian, for Genoa. It was already very hot and when we reached Alexandria where the boat was to stop two whole days, the stuffiness in the cabin was awful. Then the cranes began working right over our heads, so I had to take my husband with the help of a very kind American missionary to a hotel near the harbour where at least he could lie in a comfortable bed. He was cheerful in spite of a high fever and joked with a breezy young English doctor who came to see him. I feared we should not be able to get back on board; fortunately his temperature was better on the second day and he had a good night only disturbed by a silly incident that made him laugh heartily. No one ever locks the doors at night in the East, or at least I never did, and on that particular night at about one o'clock, when we were both fast asleep, someone entered the room and switched on the light. I sat up in bed and stared at the intruder, a prosperous-looking person in a dinner jacket and a straw hat, who, judging from his florid appearance had had a good dinner. "This is too bad!" he exclaimed in an injured tone, his round eyes bulging out of his head. "Too bad of you," I said, "this isn't your room," at which he looked so perfectly bewildered that we both laughed aloud, while the gentleman retreated in haste, banging the door after him.

Next day my husband was able to get back on board, and, in spite of two horrid days in that overheated cabin, he felt better on hearing Sicily was in sight, and could come up on deck and lie in a deck chair while the boat stopped before Catania. On arriving at Naples he felt so much better that he insisted on landing and having lunch at the "Gambrinus," whose excellent cooking was a treat after the boat fare. He was very gay, and said that merely breathing the air of Italy revived him. Two days later (we stopped at Leghorn on the way) we at last reached Genoa, a whole fortnight after leaving Beyrut. We were now to take the Simplon line to reach Aigle in the Rhone valley, from which a funicular runs up to Leysin. A weary journey for an invalid, and he felt so tired in the train we had to stop for the night at Arona on the lake. There I remember he enjoyed an excellent veal cutlet *à la Milanese* provided by a very sympathetic Italian host, and the opal waters of the lake at sunset made us forget our tribulations. On the next day we passed the Simplon tunnel rather like a nightmare. My husband felt stuffy and oppressed, and I was terribly anxious, not knowing what was awaiting us at Aigle. Only those who have travelled with an invalid know the many unforeseen difficulties that arise at every step. Besides the ready money I had was nearly finished, and I knew a cheque would have to be cashed the first thing on reaching Leysin, and would they change it without knowing us ? Our appearance was by this time far from prosperous and I knew no one at Leysin. On reaching Aigle we found we should have to spend the night there, which put the last touch to my anxiety. We managed somehow to reach Leysin the next morning, and the aspect of this haven of rest to which we had been looking forward all through those weary weeks was so terrible that my heart sank, and I tried to turn my husband's attention by talking of plans for the future, so that he should not notice the numerous châlets and hospitals for bone-patients that greet the eye of the newly-arriving, with the long rows of bed-ridden children lying in the sun. As in all these Swiss health resorts, the whole population of the place consisted of invalids in various stages of decline, which is extremely depressing for all those that are sensitive to the moral atmosphere in which they are placed. My husband found a nice room at the " Belvedere," one of the best hotels (for they were not termed sanatoriums), with a small loggia for the individual open-air cure. His experience of the Cotswold Sanatorium had been very different, and he could not understand the hotel organisation of these cure-houses leaving perfect liberty to the patients, who were visited daily by a very courteous but not particularly interested doctor attached to the establishment, and were otherwise left to take care of themselves. This method was perhaps not a bad one for those who, like my husband, had some experience of a curative diet, but in cases of utterly ignorant persons, and these were the more numerous, the results were far from satisfactory. After settling my husband in his comfortable new quarters I started in search of a room which I could only get at a small boarding house at the other end of the village. I shall never forget that dismal place or the unfortunate creatures that fought for life in it. Its description could have furnished Dante with another circle for his Inferno. Yet, in a few weeks my husband grew so much better that for both of us Leysin began to take on a different aspect, and we were very near considering it a sort of earthly Paradise—so little does reality exist outside our moods and fancies.

On my birthday I received the following first draft of the " Old Ships," which my husband had just written (it was the first poem he wrote after those he had sent off from Brumana for his volume of the " Golden Journey "). I give it here as it differs from his last version published in " Collected Poems," and contains the lines about the " caverned Cyclades," which are given as " A Fragment " in the above volume.

## FOR HELLÉ

### Written on a Happy Day—July 13th, 1913.

I have seen old ships sailing ; still alive
On those blue waters lilied by the seas
That still can tell the caverned Cyclades
The charm which heartened Peleus to his dive
That day he left his tower upon the coast
And drove right down across the darker swell
His ivory body flitting like a Ghost
And past the holes where the eyeless fishes dwell
Found his young mother thronèd in her shell.

And all these ships were old,
Painted the mid-sea blue or deep sea green,
And patterned with the vine and grapes in gold.
    But I have seen
Pointing her shadow gently to the West
And imaged fair upon her mirror bay
A ship a little older than the rest
And fading where she lay.
Who knows.   In that old ship—but in that same
(Fished up beyond Phæacia, patched as new and painted
    brighter blue)
With patient comrades sweating at the oar
That talkative, unskilful seaman came
From Troy's fire-crimson shore
And with loud lies about his Wooden Horse,
Wrapped in his eloquence, forgot his course.
It was so old a ship—who knows—who knows,
It was so beautiful—I watched in vain
To see its mast split open with a rose,
And all its timbers burst to leaf again.

————————

*British Consulate General,*
*Beyrut,*
    *Syria.*
[*Paris, Jan. 2nd*], 1913.

MY DEAR MARSH :

Your letter has come just at the last moment to
console me.   I honestly and without being merely
amiable agree in your criticisms, indeed I am not at all
sure about Act I, Scenes I and II, but they might be
exalted by making Hassan himself more exalted.   I want
to have plenty of buffoonery—but it should be universal.
I hope you will tell anyone you send it to, not to despair
till he reads past Act I, Scene II.

I shall have the 3rd Act ready in a month.   I'll leave
out the further magic scene that I had planned and try
and give the beggars a better show.

I shall anxiously await news at Beyrut.
And some people go to Syria for pleasure !
                                        Yours very sincerely,
                                                J. E. FLECKER.

                            10 *rue du Marché*,
                                        *Neuilly*,
                                                *Paris*.
[*To* MR. JOHN MAVROGORDATO]          *3rd Jan.* 1913.
    Just a chance this may get you.  If so, come and meet
at the Peiraeus if you can the big Messageries boat that
leaves Marseilles on or about the 9th, if you care to see
me.  My wife is, unfortunately, not returning to Beirut
till later.

                            Yours ever,
                                    J. E. FLECKER.

                    *Chez Madame Skiadaressi*,
                        10 *rue du Marché*,
                            *Neuilly-sur-Seine*,
                                    *France*.
                        *Sunday.  January*, 1913.

MY DEAR MARSH :
    The Foreign Office having given me an extension of
leave for a fortnight, I have fled hither for peace and
refreshment.  Before we left London we saw *Twelfth
Night*, and were quite overwhelmed by its excellence.*
    I am definitely going to be an Usher in Nottingham
next September unless, as I hope, something more
cheerful turns up.  I am writing to Benson.
    The hope of my life, which is *Hassan*, is in your
hands, my dear Marsh.  I am longing to hear what
Ainley thinks of it, still more to hear what Barker

    * *Twelfth Night* produced by Granville Barker.  The only time I saw
my husband so moved by a theatrical production, the tears rolling down his
face.

82

hears of it, and no less to hear what you think of it. Do not scruple to tell me bad news and bad opinions.

My best love to Rupert, and many thanks to you for your great kindness to one as unfortunate as Ovid.

JAMES ELROY FLECKER.

[*To* HAROLD MONRO]
*British Consulate General,*
*Beirut.*
31 *Jan.* [1913.]

DEAR MONRO :

Just got your letter. Yes, send the books to Syria I will do " John D " for the June number—I would rather. Leave out the whole verse about the behinds if you like. It was meant to make you laugh. How difficult some people are : is there no such thing as high poetic humour ? Send me a copy of Chesterton's ballad please. I warn you that I think he is the only man alive who can write a line of decent poetry now that Yeats, Kipling, A. E. Housman are silent.

I am very glad, at all events, you like the poem, and wish every success to your valiant and unselfish enterprise.

J. E. FLECKER.

How I hate exile ! Am daily waiting to get a place in England. If you hear of one let me know. Will write to Marsh—but the MS. should be being looked at by Actor Managers.

*British Consulate General,*
*Beirut,*
*Syria.*
11*th February,* 1913.

MY DEAR MARSH :

Many thanks for your long expected letter, very welcome as being from you, despite a certain amount of disappointment. Will you be so very kind as to do this for me. Shew it to Mr. John Drinkwater, if he is still desirous of seeing it, mentioning to him that the farce is going to be largely revised and exscinded, just to see if he takes an interest in it, and then return it to me. I will then do the last act.

I am at present alone here—my wife is coming next month, and forced to spend most of my spare time working for a Turkish exam. However, I have nearly completed the final revision of my novel *The King of Alsander*, which the great Secker " no-limericks-damn-you " is going to publish as soon as sent. It is such an odd work, I do not know if it will be good or bad. Have also written a few poems.

I adopted a cavilling air in my review to the *E. R.*, which I don't know if they have or will publish. I praised you as anthologist, Rupert, Davies, De la Mare. I cursed Mr. Gibson and the particular poem of Mase-field's you put in. I thought better not to be too rhapsodical, so as to avoid all appearance of insincerity.

I have not yet had any good news about getting work in England, though I have written to about a hundred people. I have hopes of the C.U. Appointments people. I should think I ought to get a secretaryship. That is the summit of my ambition. I *can't* learn enough about the stage here in Beirut to become a dramatist—even if there were no other reasons.

Yet I wish England could have ten consecutive days of hot and brilliant sunshine in February! The whole country is and has been for the last three weeks blazing with flowers.

I am very grateful to you for all the trouble you have taken : please forgive me for asking you to take this little more !

Sincerely yours,<br>J. E. FLECKER.

A GROUP OF BEDAWI CAMEL-DRIVERS.

A SMALL INN ON THE LEBANON.

[To face p. 84.

*British Consulate General,*
*Beyrut.*
*April 20th.* [1913.]

MY DEAR MONRO :

Here is " John Davidson." I never knew quite what you wanted of me : I only hope this will please you. It has been written under great difficulties, as I have been ill for several weeks : however, I am now better and frantically trying to come back from exile.

Many thanks for sending me the *Poetry Review* and printing *The Golden Journey*. As for the John Davidson books, I will send them all back, but would like to keep the *Selections* only.

I should like to challenge Mr. Flint to quote a single line of Paul Claudel that has the slightest merit whatever. It is certainly not the little thoughts on God that are going to impress anybody. He is the French Ella Wheeler Wilcox, only far more poisonously pretentious, and much duller.

I am publishing, as you may know, my new volume of poems under the title of *The Golden Journey to Samarkand*, with a passionate preface against fools and all who do not admire the Parnassian theory of verse.

Is not Chesterton's *White [Wild] Knight* reissued ? If so, please send me a copy.

Please acknowledge the receipt of this by return.

Yours sincerely,
J. E. FLECKER.

*Hotel Belvédère,*
*Leysin-sur-Aigle,*
*Switzerland.*
*June 5th* [1913]

MY DEAR MONRO :

Severe illness, which was already coming on, when I somewhat feverishly wrote you " John Davidson," has driven me here. This place, however, is rapidly curing me—but an end to the purple East! Henceforward, infinite poverty—a cottage, and a pen! Sheer ill-health has driven me to the literary career.

I suppose you disliked "John Davidson"—for I hoped greatly for a line of receipt from you and never got one. If you didn't dislike it and printed it, please send me copy of *Poetry and Drama* (why didn't you call it "Serres & Drama") also an infinite cheque for it and the *Golden Journey*, to buy a Cottage Piano with.

I have sent off this auspicious day corrected proofs of my new volume *The Golden Journey to Samarkand*. I have put all my power up to the last moment in making the book absolutely major poetry from beginning to end (tho' it does contain "Bryan of Brittany"), and I am immensely proud of it, and of course it will fail.

Write to me a line at all events and let me know how the great cause is getting on!

Ever yours,

J. E. FLECKER.

> *Hotel Belvédère,*
> *Leysin-sur-Aigle,*
> *Switzerland.*
> *June 5th.* [1913.]

MY DEAREST FRANK:

I have fallen ill again and have left the purple East, thank God, for ever. I nearly died on the voyage—seeing Sicily, Naples, Genoa, and the lakes and the Simplon pass as some awful and unholy dream with a perpetual temperature of 104. 6 days of this place has sent my temperature down to normal, and there being nothing very seriously wrong with my lung (only the old spot touched up again by an influenza) I hope to be well again in a few months. But then weakness and delicateness of constitution will force me to live—as my people now want me to live, in some Devonshire or South Coast cottage, and write.

I am soon bringing out my 2nd volume of poems called *The Golden Journey to Samarkand*. I have spared no pains to make it absolute major poetry from end to end, and I think it challenges any volume of verse published since *Atalanta in Calydon*—yea, even *The Shropshire Lad* and *The Wind Among the Reeds*. A mad publisher has paid me £10 in advance of royalties, but I suppose I shall sell 70 copies, and *The Times* will say my verse is musical and harmonious. We are almost near one another. How I long to see you again. Please write to me. I have written little not from forgetfulness, but always with the hope of seeing you at last.

Ever yours,<br>JAMES.

*Hotel Belvédère,*
*Leysin-sur-Aigle,*
*Switzerland.*
*June 5th, 1913.*

MY DEAR MARSH :
Your kind letter was forwarded on from Beirut and I received it yesterday. My health broke down in Beirut, and I am spending the summer here. I almost perished on the voyage, and thought my fragile life was ended, but now after a week the marvellous air of this very horrid place has set me well on the way to convalescence. No more of the infernal East for me, at all events. I am going to live in a very small cottage and write—it's nearly the only thing I'm fit to do ; though I may perhaps get an appointment on the *Near East*.

I have to-day sent off the corrected proofs of my new volume *The Golden Journey to Samarkand* : I am immensely proud of the volume, which is about twice as good as the

42 poems, and I feel it ought to redeem me from the stigma of minor poetry for ever. I suppose it will sell about 75 copies, and *The Times* will call it a volume of " musical and harmonious verse."

I wish they would make Rudyard Kipling Poet Laureate, like sensible people. I have a horror of their giving it to that fellow Watson, who has exactly the amount of initiative melody and second-rate imagination that captivates the Stock Exchange or Parliament.

I hope Drinkwater will read *Hassan* soon, for it takes but half-an-hour. Then if you send it me with his remarks I may be well enough to set about the revision and the completion of the 3rd Act.

My love to Rupert if he be with you. Saw a photo of you in some old illustrated the other day, sitting behind Winston.

P.S.—Please ask the Editor of *Rhythm or Blue Review* to send me a copy here, I have never seen one.


> *Hotel Belvédère,*
> *Leysin,*
> *Switzerland.*
> *June 6th,* 1913.

*To* EDWARD MARSH

On second thoughts would you be so kind as to rescue for me the MS. of *Hassan* and sent it me at once. I cannot find my MS. of Act I. (It's packed somewhere) and as life is beginning to stir within me and I've got nothing on earth to do but lie in bed all day feeling pretty well (shall be up in a day or two), I have determined to seize the opportunity, and finish and revise *Hassan*. I am going to cut the farce clean out—or modify it greatly, and be less heavy with the oriental expressions.

On the other hand, I shall not worry over much about

the requisites of the Stage. A lot of rot is talked about literary plays not succeeding. It usually means that plays which are written in lifeless blank verse on Boadicea or Savonarola, and which are infinitely boring to read, are not good stage plays. *Strafford* is not a good stage play—but then it is rather a bad poem—and certainly a dull one. I am only going to try and keep *Hassan* interesting : then if it's good enough, the stage can adapt it or adapt itself to it. It will be much better for Drinkwater and Barker to read my final version after all. I am also going to revise my other play *Don Juan ;* I talked to you about it perhaps. Bernard Shaw read it and was complimentary, but it's still a very crude production.

J. E. F.

*Hotel Belvédère,*
*Leysin,*
*Switzerland.*
17 *June,* 1913.

MY DEAR MARSH :

Forgive a postcard in reply to all your kindness, but I'm not quite up to a letter.

I received *Hassan* safely and the very encouraging letter from Birmingham, which has set me to work at once on revising and completing the play. The farce with the Jew has gone clean out at once.

I can't write much per day, but heavens, I've got time and leisure enough for anything.

Will you permit me to present you when it comes out with the only copy of the " Edition de Luxe " of my poems that I am going to give away ? That is, if the publisher keeps his promise to print an Edition de Luxe.

Yours sincerely,
J. E. FLECKER.

P.S.—I favour Kipling, as you may have seen.

*Hotel Belvédère,*
*Leysin-sur-Aigle,*
*Switzerland,*
[*Received June* 21, 1913]

MY DEAR OLD FRANK:

A letter reaches you in a day : it makes one long to see you—and I would urge you to come here were the place not so horrible in itself (being all full of invalids) for anyone doing a holiday. If I shift up into the Tyrol later then you *must* come.

You see how badly I want you. First of all for yourself. Secondly to talk about all the good things of the world—such as riding, sailing (to be damn manly, like Masefield : I've shamelessly cribbed your excellent epithet in a dig at him in the preface to the *Golden Journey*)—and most especially Henri de Régnier, Samain, and Paul Fort, and the great French Poets of the last forty years for whom (see again my Preface) I am conceiving an astonishing admiration.

How sick I am of reading! I am going to get boxes of stone bricks, to practise architecture. But above all I am going to write to Geneva for a toy theatre to work *Hassan* on. For I'm hard at work finishing *Hassan of Bagdad*—an Oriental play. The first 2 acts have been shown to the manager of the new Birmingham repertory theatre, who has written enthusiastically. But I should prefer Granville Barker, who has promised to read the play.

I wrote in *Daily News* urging Kipling as Laureate and reminding the b——s that a Court Poet didn't mean a bad poet as James Douglas seemed to think.

Have just read an old volume of Chesterton Essays called *Tremendous Trifles*. I love Chesterton : he is a man of whom one does not soon tire. His ideas on life are exactly mine. Those silly frogs believe that Kings, Lords and Snobs can rescue them from their welter of pornography and restore " religion, faith and the army."

The silly Parisians never looked outside their capital, where they will find all these three requisites in excellent state—supported by a democratic peasantry.

Of course I don't agree with Chesterton (or you it seems) about religion—and that's a long story.

Well, here I lie, and as Chesterton suggests the best thing for a man to do lying in bed would be to have a very long brush to paint with on the ceiling (though the colours would fall in his face). After all I've got heaps of time to write—as never in my life before : and I'm very slowly getting better.

Hope you can read this scrawl. A long letter from you would be the best thing in the world. The last was too short.

Thine ever<br>JAMES.

Belvédère,<br>Leysin,<br>5th July.

MY DEAR FRANKO :

I have just received a telegram from you—rather mysterious—which I presume means that my book is out (I have not yet got my own copy) and that you like it. It is most charming of you to send me such a wire : but I impatiently await a letter—for you know your judgment is with Jack's and as I now add my wife's, one of the only three judgments which mean to me anything at all : though there is something also to be said for the critic of the *Athenæum*.

Daily I meant to write in answer to your last—but put it off till my book came out. I read carefully the Conrad which with the 50 cent stamp (you should have asked me for stamps when I was in Beirut) I return. You have taken a very subtle and excellent point about Conrad and worked it out—but wasn't there more to say? Only I don't see how one could say it except lyrically. The exotic part is marvellous : the passion of *Youth* is something one can only write poems on. But Conrad is never English. His novels have to be corrected. (I know the man who did it.) His novels have never attracted the English public (who are bloody fools—but I think it's something deeper) and poor Conrad has now as you know a Civil list pension. You read *Under Western Eyes* about those Russians ? But I wonder no more at Russian novels : they are about Russians, and Russians are such queer fish you've only got to photograph them to produce an apparent work of psychological genius.

FRANCIS THOMPSON. Jack utterly loathes him as a quack. I have been forced to admire " The Hunched Camels " and some other bits they've been quoting in the papers. But he is a quack.

Of French Poets, do buy and read

1. Paul Fort : " Vivre en Dieu."
2. Henri de Régnier : "Les jeux rustiques et divins."
3. Samain : "Le Jardin de l'Infante or Aux flancs du Vase."
4. Moréas : " Stances."

The first two are alive—and more living. Henri de Régnier is marvellous beyond anything ever written— for subtlety and (read the " Warrior's Gate ") for strength, Paul Fort is a joyish boyish Chesterton person (it rhymes you think it don't but it do). The " Férté Milon " is what you read out of his volume. You must read French poetry : it is so infinitely the finest left in the world.

Read too Claude Farrerè's novel *La Bataille*—procurable for 1fr.50, about Japan, very powerful and fascinating.

*Concerning a saying of yours* implying no decent man would care to get to know Malays and wandering Arabs—don't follow Chesterton into the anti-Oriental fallacy. Eastern races are worth knowing—or we should never have had either Burton or Kipling, both very decent men. (I re-read much Kipling : *They* is beyond all praise—and the half-humorous poetry is my delight.)

Concerning A—— N——. Why? Frank. He is a vile ass. You might as well suggest Hall Caine for the O.M. It is going I hear to Robert Bridges—a dull person but more respectable. If not Kipling, why not Newbolt? What asses people are.

I have got my *toy theatre* and play with it all day. I shall send you *Hassan* as soon as it is finished; I've still half an act to do. All my hopes are on it. It's utterly Oriental externally, but I hope the flash of the little European blood I possess gleams through its seraglio atmosphere from time to time !

G—— b—— the Bulgars : and I think he will. They are entirely and absolutely greedy swine.

Am much better and walking. Am going to a little 5—7 franc pension lone lone in the country for August. *Is there any chance of your coming along for a fortnight?* Do come and play with the toy theatre and talk *Hassan* and walk. The fare's not much I imagine, and the place is high up and healthy if it has no other advantage.

Please don't punish my laziness by keeping me waiting for a letter as long as I've kept you.

Ever thine<br>JAMES.

*Hotel Belvédère,*<br>*Leysin,*

*July 15th, 1913.*

MY DEAR MARSH :

I am sending you a copy of *The Golden Journey* this mail. I think its clothes, for which my publisher is entirely responsible, are rather jolly.

I was simply delighted to have your enthusiastic letter. I am glad you like the *Gates of Damascus*. I consider it my best work. Of course *Diarbekir* should

have a note. It is known as the " black city " throughout
the East on account of the dark stone of its walls.
" Mountains " it ought to be in Brumana of course ; I
had already noticed this irritating slip and sent to
Goschen to print an " erratum."

I think I would not have inserted Phaeacia or the
Sacred Incident if I had had time to revise the book
thoroughly or write more poems.

The original of Cyclamen as horned, etc., was honied
cyclamen, as white as death if you like that better. I
don't think my ear objects to these very mild resolutions
of the metre. I cannot—with all deference—get to like
the " Golden Road " as much as the " Golden Journey " :
I wouldn't mind " Golden *Track* " so much.

I hope you will get a chance of reviewing me somewhere !

Many thanks for getting people to buy the book !

Ever yours,

James Elroy Flecker.

> *Hotel Staphani,*
> *Montana-sur-Sierre,*
> *Switzerland.*

Dear Monro :          *7th September* [1913].

Hope *Poetry and Drama* will give my poems a review.
Do send me the June and September Nos. and put me
down as a subscriber.

We must remember, said a reviewer of me in the
*Standard*, that " after the Parnassians came Baudelaire and
Richelieu."

That naughty young contemporary Frenchman
Baudelaire !

Claudel *is* rot : I read it. Flint thinks I'm rot, so it
doesn't matter. *Don't* let him review me. Best wishes
for all your undertakings : please send me De la Mare's
" Peacock Pie."

James Elroy Flecker.

13.10.13.

MY DEAR MARSH :

If you happen to be writing please write to me at :—

> Pension Alexandra,
> Montreux-Territet,
> Switzerland.

I hope to stay here some weeks. The change has improved my temper and done no harm to my health. Then back to the beastly mountains for the Winter season.

—— tells me *Georgian Poetry* is in its 7th edition. Congratulating.

> Ever yours,
> JAMES ELROY FLECKER.

> *Hotel Belvédère,*
> *Leysin,*
> *Switzerland.*
> *Monday,* 5. VIII. 13.

MY DEAR MARSH :

It was delightful of you to send the letter from Gosse to me. My heartiest thanks. As a matter of fact Gosse could have discovered me himself had he liked, for with the insolence of youth I remember sending him years ago a copy of the *Bridge of Fire.*

I have also had a charming letter from Raleigh, to whom I sent a copy (but not a luxe copy) of my book.

The reviews have been few. An excellent one in the *Globe*—but mentioning that he would prefer " Golden Road " to " Golden Journey " on account of the extra metric syllable. I bow to criticism, and have just amended journey to road in the copy of the poem which ends the last act of *Hassan.*

For *Hassan* is finished. I am sending it to London to be typed this week, and I will, if you still hold to your generous offer of looking after it, send it you as soon as typed. I have terrible high hopes of it, and I shall suffer undoubtedly terrible disappointment. Yet, Heavens, when I read the text of *Kismet*, which I have just unearthed from a Geneva Library, and think of the success which that extraordinary piffle (puérilité grave si chère à l'âme anglo-saxonne, said a French critic) that stuff so devoid of invention, so feeble even in the crudest dramatic tricks, I can but hope that some day *Hassan* will be staged.

I am very angry with *The Times*. It has again given me a two-line review. These two-line reviews do not exclude further notice, but it was all I got for the " 42." Do you, dear Marsh, know the wretch who doles me out two lines of faint approbation, and could you persuade him to damn the book if he likes, but at least to take it seriously.

I hope *Rhythm* and *Poetry and Drama* will give me decent reviews. Does *Rhythm* want me? I am so sick of having one poem out of five taken by the *Nation*, and one a year printed in the *English Review*, that I should like to cast in my lot with the other children—if they want me.

Meanwhile I've been told off by the *Near East* to write on the Balkans. It's healthy to interest oneself in other things than dreams.

Do write again, your letters are so welcome.

Yours ever,

JAMES ELROY FLECKER.

*Hotel Belvédère,*
*Leysin,*
*Switzerland.*
*Saturday.*

MY DEAR MARSH:
I certainly was surprised to receive the cheque this morning: it is most generous of you to divide your

profits among your poets. Many thanks : I will devote it to getting *Hassan* beautifully typed. For *Hassan* is now two scenes off completion.

There is to be an edition de luxe* : it is already out, but the silly people, despite my warning, are sending me my copies by parcel post, which will take a day or two. I am going to send you your copy from here : so I'm afraid it may be a few days late.

Meanwhile, if you see my book let me have your candid opinion. I should much value your criticism.

Granville Barker's sister has left here for England to-day.

Ever yours,

J. E. FLECKER.

*Hotel Belvédère,*
*Leysin.*
*Saturday* [*July,* 1913.]

MY DEAREST FRANKO :

Ever so many thanks for your letter of criticism. Hellé told me particularly to tell you that she agreed with you practically in everything. So do I. I think you underrate *Santorin*—much admired by Dunsany, by the way. *Lord Arnaldos* was after all a translation. Otherwise I agree with you, particularly in your damnations. I might explain that the Publishers wrote asking if I had anything for them at once and I very hurriedly replied— nothing but a new volume of poetry. I packed off a weird collection of stuff to make up a volume including a revision of " The Bridge of Fire." I then sat down to write the book—and it was *after I got the proofs* I managed to hoof out all sorts of godless rot, and replace them by " In Hospital," " Brumana," " Taoping " ; and also

---

* Of the *Golden Journey to Samarkand.*

just at the last minute I suddenly rewrote " The Gates of Damascus " and enlarged it. There are still two rotten poems in the book—" Phaeacia " (an unconscious imitation of Yeats and Jack Beazley) and the " Sacred Incident "—both of which I should, however, describe as harmless rather than offensive.

It may amuse you to know a little of the history of these things : you certainly deserve to be told if it amuses you.

1. " The Preface " : Written when I was pretty ill—like all the later poems—is not quite sincere. My chief desire was to say what I thought was wanted to shake up the critics : not to expound the essence of poetry, which would take 500 pages. The beginning is ugly enough with " theory " repeated so often—but I re-read the end with pleasure and thank you for the word " manly."

2. The Epilogue is the last scene of *Hassan*—or rather I wrote *Hassan* to lead up to the Epilogue. A moonlight scene, a sudden burst into poetry (you know my trick from *Don Juan*), and the singer with the beautiful voice is the chief character of the play—the famous singer Ishak—*anima naturaliter christiana*. If it doesn't give the public shivers down the back when it is acted in its place, I'll never write again.

3. " The Gates of Damascus." I consider this to be my greatest poem—and I am glad you seem to agree. It was inspired by Damascus itself by the way. I loathe the East and the Easterns, and spent all my time there dreaming of Oxford. Yet is seems—even to hardened Orientalists—that I understand.

4. " Yasmin " is an anthology piece. It is part of *Hassan*—written for it and should sound well in its place.

5. " Saadabad " is with " Areiya " perhaps the only poem with individual passion I have written. Though verses 1, 3 and 4, of Part I are translations from the

Turkish, the poem is the most passionately sincere I have ever written. It was written straight out and not a line revised.

6. Of course the " Turkish Lady " won't wash. The poem is a pretty close translation in the book.

7. " Doris," dear Frank—it's very short and I don't think it's easy to say how sincere. Might come out of the Greek anthology. I mean by the Ship the Ship of Dreams.

8. Glad you like " Hyali." I never saw the island (which exists) but I passed it in the night—and I have seen many isles of the Ægean.

9. Don't you think the *Legend* at least of " Santorin " one of the loveliest in the world ? I wonder if you weird Catholics realize that the Middle Age is still in flower in the Ægean. " That man married a Syren " said a peasant once to my wife—and showed the man !

10. " A Ship an Isle " you don't mention. A very subtle poem, Frank, and when you read Henri de Régnier you will find some more.

11. " Oak and Olive." A jest after all in the good old manner. No, I wouldn't have it out of the volume though, of course, it's very slight.

12. " Brumana." Horrible misprint—in lines you quoted—*mountain* should be *mountains*. Poem sincere enough, good God, was thinking of the *Bournemouth pines*. Lavdanon is the Greek name of the cytisus, a rock rose which makes the woods lovely in Syria. It has a queer little scent.

13. " Areiya " was, as it says, written in three minutes and never altered.

14. My wife likes " Bryan " ; I hate it—or rather find it cold. But the story (a Greek story again), is jolly enough.

15. Damn clever of me to write a poem as far out of myself as the " Painter's Mistress." My wife has not

ceased wondering. Suggested by a play of Bataille's and written on the Lebanon.

16. Oh, I did sweat when very ill over " Taoping," and turned it from rot into a good poem of workmanship. Suggested by a strange amazing book of one Daguerches, called " *Consolata fille du Soleil.*" . . .

Concerning the Chinese. Frank, I almost accuse you of insincerity. Do you really shudder at a Japanese print ? Do you really believe in the " inhuman oriental " myth ? Or do you think you ought to believe in the myth ?

Don't you think that the healthy honest way for a European to look at a Chinaman or a nigger is to laugh at him ? Don't you think they are there for the joy of the picturesque—as I portray them in " Taoping " ?

The Turks, too. I hate them because I am a modern civilised man. Catholics should and do love them. Why is Turkey rotten ? Why is the Turk an inefficient gentleman ? Islam ? Nonsense : not entirely. Simply because he thinks middle age and is middle age. Saladin and Richard were both very near each other. They talked the same language. They both believed in Aristotle. But Saladin is still Saladin—arguing with a twist—because his *Aristotle* was translated for him and he never learnt Latin at the Renaissance. Richard is now King George V. . . .

Do read Paul Fort. Perhaps the greatest of all French poets. The humour is wonderful. Have just read *Mortcerf* and an introduction which quotes the most amazingly jolly things.

1. " *Du temps qu'on allait encore aux baleines, si loin que Ca faisait, mat'lot, pleurer vos belles, y avait sur chaque route un Jésus en croix, y avait des marquis couverts de dentelles, y avait la Sainte Vierge et y avait le Roi.*"

2. " *Du temps qu'on allait encore aux baleines, si loin que Ca faisait mat'lot pleurer les belles, y avait des marins qui*

*avaient la foi et des grands seigneurs qui crachaient sur elle et
y avait la Sainte Vierge et y avait le Roi."*

3. " *Eh bien, à présent tout le monde est content, c'est pas
pour dire mat'lot mais on est content ! y a plus de grands
seigneurs ni de Jésus qui tiennent, y a la République et y a
l'Président et y a plus de baleines."*

That should send you round to the bookshop.

So sorry you have neuralgia ! hope you are better.

*Hassan* nearly ended. You shall see it when complete.

Write again soon as your letters are a great joy.

I don't believe in Barbey's Catholicism a bit. See
Jules Lemaître on him.

Thine,

JAMES.

*Pension Alexandra,
Montreux,
Switzerland.*

MY DEAR MARSH :

Alas, you too will cease to love me, if I importune
you. However honestly it's about time to make a move
about *Hassan*. But I don't want to worry you about
that pestilent Oriental. Will you only be good enough
to give me the address of Barker's reader A. E. Drinkwater. You see he's had it 2 months and if every
Manager keeps it 2 months it will be about 15 years
before anything happens ! I ought at least to have had
a word saying the MS. was under consideration. It's a
pest not having another MS. but I could send a MS.
to John Drinkwater—only I do want to try London
first.

I have heard from Francis. What *is* he doing in the
Victoria and Albert ? Francis in an Art gallery is simply
too odd an idea for words.

Very glad to see that Gosse is named officier of the Légion d'honneur. Am puzzled at times why he hasn't received more honour in his own country. You know I got a letter to Paul Fort from him.

I like " Peacock Pie."

Do you know anything of a boy or young man vaguely at or formerly at Cambridge ? He wrote me a nice letter—all letters of appreciation are nice but his was rather a clever one—and it seems he is a poet.

Are you going to volunteer for Ulster ? Oh I *do* wish they would fight.

Ever yours,
JAMES ELROY FLECKER.

P.S.—Do forgive me being a pestilential nuisance. Poets with plays are a horrid bore, but managers who keep 'em three months and return them with a printed notice of regret are even worse.

A letter from you is sure to miss this.

*Pension Villa Alexandra,*
*Montreux-Territet,*
*Switzerland.*
*[August,* 1913.]

MY DEAR MARSH :
Many thanks for your letter which I got just after sending you the card. I don't think G. Barker ought to hate me. It was only the last postcard sent about a week ago that was unduly importunate : the other letters simply gave my address, in case he wanted to write to me direct.

I suppose one must believe (this is just a reflection on general grounds) in the enormous business of a Theatre Manager. Arnold Bennett doesn't, I believe, and said so somewhere. But begosh, as one might say,

I don't think much of the business-like attainments of the Press, I have had so little experience, yet it already counts. . . .

Horrors ! You'll think I'm grumbling again. I'm only amusing you with Tales, Olden Tales. My God, if one ran a Consulate on these lines ! Goldring has told me dreadful stories of the experiences of other poor devils.

I'll send a copy to Drinkwater if you think advisable, but I'd like to get Barker's opinion first. I would have written to Barker's reader (is it a relation to the other Drinkwater ?) but don't know his address.

I enclose a new version of God save the King. I can't make up my mind if it's rather good or a joke or both. It wants a final verse on the Mother Country. Then I think I'd better send it to George and publish it in *The Times*.

Ever yours,
J. E. FLECKER.

This place is divine after the Mountains. What *is* Rupert doing in Canada ? and why does Monro condescend to print sniffs against Kipling and Tennyson. Does he really imagine any of the stuff he has published (mine or anyone else's) is up to the level of those great men.

*Hotel de Glion,*
*Glion-sur-Montreux,*
*Switzerland.*
*Aug.* 14*th.* 13.

MY DEAR FRANK :

Forgive a postcard just to give you my new permanent address. I have been ordered to this lower summer and incomparably more delightful place. One can see

*Sanatorium Stephani,*
*Montana-sur-Sierre,*
*Switzerland.*
28.8.13.

DEAR MARSH :

I hope you've got *Hassan*.  Above address is, I hope, permanent.  Do let me know your own opinion of *Hassan*.  I hope you'll have time to show it to Barker before you go to Spain.

Do forgive a postcard as I've been travelling and am very tired.

Yours ever,
JAMES ELROY FLECKER.

*Sanatorium Stephani,*
*Montana-sur-Sierre,*
1*st* [*recd. Sept.* 3/13.]

MY DEAR FRANK :

I prefer to write as letters are very quick and I've just time to catch the post.

*Certainly* show it to your friend.  Certainly let it be translated if there's any chance of it being *played*.  But it can't be published till after it's played in England— if it ever is.  Try and get it taken by a German theatre by all means.  Only I know you will only show it to honourable men and friends of yours.  It seems people are very apt to collar foreign plays without acknowledgement.  If the play were published in Germany someone would go and play it without asking leave and to take action would be absurdly difficult.  But do let me know what your friend thinks, and do let him read it.

In fearful and incoherent haste.

JAMES.

*Sana. Stephani,*
*Montana-sur-Sierre,*
*Switzerland.*
*[recd. Sept. 5/13.]*

MY DEAR OLD FRANK :

Jolly to get the 1st criticisms of *Hassan* from you.
I am quite lost now, having nothing to work at, and at
times have a wild idea of trying to make a masterpiece
out of that hopeless *Don Juan.*

Rum. Act IV. Sc. 4, was written with great passion,
except possibly the concluding scene, and we both of
us wept when we read it. I think the end wants mending.
Pervaneh is philosophising—I tried to make it ecstatic—
but it's as preachy as Bernard Shaw. But again she is
rather a cold fine woman (or I meant her to be)—a sort
of brave cowardly noble beast.

The part of the play that thrills me most is the ghosts—
and don't you think the effect of the poem at the end
should be grand. I love my ghosts—I suppose because
my poetic soul loves the picturesque in the play above
everything.

Hassan originally was going to try and whip Yasmin
not to kill her. But I decided that would be too sadistic,
and not serious enough so I altered it. I'm fond of the
little scene of Yasmin and the Executioner.

I am pleased with myself, my dear Frank, as usual.
*Hassan* is, I think, supremely stageable and written with
a certain consistency and polish which Tristan Bernard,
or one of those clever Frenchmen might not be ashamed
of. An oriental play must be a spectacle of course. But
of the scenes two come twice (street with fountain and
Caliph's garden) one is a mere painted drop scene
(outside the cell) and the first scene of all and the Caliph's
divan are simple interiors. What will be expensive are
the dresses and the camel. *Kismet* (I've read the muck
in French) was far more exacting.

making terms I won't stick out for about a thousand quid myself.

You may assure him that while I won't take less than £20 I won't ask for more *unless* the piece has been played in England with success. In that case, too, I will be advised by you, and you may rely on me to be sensible. Will you please thank Herr Freissler for me and tell him how sensible I am of the honour he is doing me. Tell him also to be just as free with the text as he likes—to omit add or alter anything to make it better drama or better German. I am not at all touchy on these matters, and when I make a translation I mutilate the original horribly with a view to improvement. Should Herr Freissler care, his translation finished, to attempt to place the play (especially if it gets played in England with any success) in a theatre, I will willingly constitute him my agent in the matter : for it would be more profitable for both of us than a thousand editions or publications.

Coming down from the clouds, I'm a poor and excessively needy devil who never expects *Hassan* to be played anywhere, and would be hellish glad of twenty quid and will have to restrain myself from writing once a week to Herr Freissler to urge him to buck up and get it done.

You are wickedly and obstinately silent about two things.

A. You *will* not read Paul Fort, on whom I am going to write an article and shall want your opinion. Try *Coxcomb*. It's rather blasmous but very wonderful.

Secondly, you won't say a word or even make a decent excuse about coming here for a week about Xmas. None of the other hotels accept any lungs as this is a Sport place and it will be simply hearty british in the Winter. The Loetschberg makes it a damn easy journey.

Ever yours, O spreader of my continental reputation,
JAMES.

*Stephani,*
*Montana.*
*24th [Sept.]*

MY DEAR FRANK:

Herr Freissler wrote to me about *Hassan*, and I've just replied after a masterful struggle with the German. You will see what I wrote. Am too exhausted to write you a letter. I hope I haven't bullied you too much about Paul Fort. I dislike " Vivre en Dieu "—but love " La Ferté Milon," and Walter Scott in the " Manor House." Is not the exquisite poem " Philomel " in the volume *Coxcomb*? I have been very bored of life lately : only slightly buoyed up by an autograph letter from the Greek Minister in London thanking me for the Hellenic letters to the papers. Not a word about *Hassan* yet. I've got the stamp for you and some others which I will send when I write a letter. The Swiss stamps are to be changed in January next year. It's a bitter world : Edmund Gosse has a high opinion of Madame de Noailles. The business about Langen and the stage rights is a bit complicated. I ought to know what percentage they want. I have probably muddled Freissler for ever in my answer. Suppose they say to me we have got the great Actor Manager Herr Bühnenentefuss to take your noble drama. Our percentage as Agents is 80 per cent. of what you get from Herr Bühnenentefuss. I suppose I ought to worry about these things, they bore me because the joy of having *Hassan* played in any language seems very remote. Yet I ought to provide against the shadowy day of prosperity. Would you like me to send you 2 vols. of Henri de Régnier ? Help Herr Freissler to understand what I've written.

Ever thine,

JAMES.

have liked "Pannyra" which is by Samain: the "Gate of the Armies" is by Henri de Régnier. Did *you get the vol. of de Régnier I sent you?* You don't mention him. Paul Fort has sent me a copy of his new *Choix*, 600 packed pages extracted from his work (6 francs)— a marvellous book which I am plodding through. But I am too gay to read or write much now: this place agrees with me: I crawl about over the hills and am feeling quite alive again. I have written a new version of "God Save the King" which I will send you some day.

Ever yours very lazily,<br>
JAMES.

Write here: hope to stay here till Nov. 15th.

*Pension Alexandra.  Sat.*

MY DEAR FRANCO:

Delighted to get your letter. Had been saying only yesterday that life was wrong without a letter from you. The appreciations in Henri de Régnier were my wife's who tells me to tell you she's glad you're of the same opinion. But really Frank it's quite *shameless* not to have read Hérédia. The only other man who dared confess it to me was the editor of the *English Review!* Gosse in a letter to me calls de Régnier a cloudy genius: but by God it is genius and a damn fine cloud and if you don't like the "Gate of the Armies" and the "Gate of the Courtesans" you'll lose your soul. de R. married Hérédia's daughter and there's a sweet skit by La Jeunesse on Hérédia's horror on hearing an odelette by his son-in-law which actually dared to contain an idea. (The gold came from Langen's the other day and we drank your health and to a meeting at Locarno.) We have had here 20 days consecutive brilliant sunshine and I swear I'm beginning to love the country round Montreux. Am scratching this and smoking a delicious cheap cigar on a bed of dry leaves on Mount Pélerin with a glorious view and feeling quite happy. Also am frittering. There are so many funiculars railways and steamboats that one can crawl about the country like a well man, almost. I doubt if the Italian lake scenery is really as fine as this. Am scribbling my Paul Fort article at intervals. What *does* Paul Fort think of God. I confess I could hardly say. Get the 6 franc anthology if you're rich enough : it's the best 6 franc worth in the world. *Choix* it's called.

Thine ever,<br>JAMES.

*Pension Alexandra,*<br>
*Montreux.*<br>
[20.10.13].

DEAR FRANK :

Still here. Caught cold day before going back and am still in bed, but progressing. Expected to receive long letters about meaning of bits of *Hassan* from Freissler : quite disappointed. Can get *nothing* out of Barker not even the *MS. ;* my Maecenas I have asked to send a messenger boy for it. Have just read the " Colline inspirée " and have composed an anti-catholic song to irritate you with when I see you—if I ever do O Frank. I tell you one gets quite mad for the want of a little civilized society. There is a South African Jew here who asked my wife yesterday if the afterglow of the sunset wasn't what they called the Aurora Borealis.

Do write (here) : I'm rather cheerless.

JAMES.

*Pension Alexandra,*<br>
*Montreux,*<br>
*Nov. 6th,* 1913.

MY DEAR MARSH :

The boy's name is *Davey !* Sorry I omitted this interesting detail. Thanks so much for writing : *Hassan* was preying on my mind. What is the new Georgian enterprise. Francis whispered a word about new editions of *Georgian Poetry*. My patriotic poem you say less about which is probably better.

A lot of jolly people must pass through Montreux like Abercrombie. Wish the deuce I could meet someone to talk to intelligently. I haven't met a soul outside my family to talk to since I breakfasted with you and Rupert. My wits are getting absolutely mouldy and I never write a line of verse.

Ever yours,<br>
JAMES ELROY FLECKER.

P.S.—Your letter happily escaped the Melun disaster in which much correspondence addressed to me perished.

*Hotel Stephani,*<br>
*Montana-sur-Sierre.*<br>
*13th*, 11.13.

MY DEAR MARSH :

Off to the above accursed address to-morrow. The Indian Summer is over. Here is a card of the prettiest town in Switzerland, which we visited lately. Very sorry to leave Montreux, but the weather has turned. Have you read the 6 franc anthology of Paul Fort ? Have been writing a long article on him. Proofs of my novel have arrived. The novel is really much better than I thought it was. Very patchy, but jolly purplers. Hope you'll agree with this when you see it. Please when you next write give me the address of the *New Statesman*, if you happen to take it in.

Yours ever,<br>
JAMES E. FLECKER.

P.S.—What *are* Skis ?

> *Hotel Stephani,*
> *Montana-sur-Sierre,*
> *Switzerland.*
> *Nov. 26th,* 1913.

MY DEAR MARSH :

Have managed to get back to this horrible hole this
time. It will be my address for many months now. If
you know any good but healthy men, who want to
Winter sport tell 'em to come here—it's one of the
best places (no hotels but mine take invalids) with
lakes. If you have written to Montreux I shall
get the letter : Mavrogordato tells me he has sent
you the other MS., so no need to wrest the other from
G. Barker.

A letter of mine *should* appear in next *Near East,*
and might amuse you if the Balkans charm you at all.
It is intended to pulverize Aubrey Herbert and Marma-
duke Pickthall.*

> Yours ever,
> JAMES ELROY FLECKER.

P.S.—Just got yours. Of course let Barker keep it.
Mavro thinks *Tree* a likely man but do as you think right
with 2nd copy. No harm to show it round a bit. Many
thanks for all your trouble and letter to me. J. E. F.

> *Sanatorium Stephani,*
> *Station Climatérique de*
> *Montana s/Sierre*
> *(Suisse).*
> *1st December,* 1913.

MY DEAR MARSH,

I thought you might care to see the enclosed which
I wrote some months ago. As you suggested my

---

* Both eloquent apologists for the Turks.

sending you some poems for Jack Squire, perhaps
you might send this on to him, if you think it good
enough.

I'm devilish busy trying to make my novel a little
less crude at the last moment, and really I have polished
it fine. I tremble to think of the printer's bill for altered
proofs.

Though the snow is not yet fixed or thick enough for
sport, the mountain winter has begun. Much as I hate
the Alps on principle I must admit that sunset and
sunrise and moonlight on the snows, and the sea of
cloud beneath one give amazing stage effects.

My nice letter was, I suppose, too late for this week's
*Near East*.

I am fairly well but have to stay in bed. I'm so busy
with my novel however I don't mind—and when *that's*
done, the job to finish an article on Paul Fort.

I meant to ask you a rather delicate question, as it
reveals my absurd conceit. Harold Monro said last
year that somebody had " suggested " me for the
Academy's £100 prize for the 42 poems. I don't suppose
there's the slightest chance for the *Golden Journey* and
it's damned impertinence of me to think there is, but
nevertheless I should like to know if it is usual to send
books in for it, so to speak (*e.g.* to send a copy, without
a letter) to the members as if one entered oneself for
competition, or whether the said Academy are presumed
to have read everything and judge from what they have
read.

I departed from prejudice and read an English " clever
novel " the other day. It was by Violet Hunt, a practised hand, and called *The Doll*. For sheer crudeness
and bad technical workmanship I have never seen
anything like it, except perhaps the early drafts of the
*King of Alsander*.

Ever yours,
J. E. FLECKER.

> *Stephani,*
> *Montana.*
> *Saturday.*

[*To* FRANK SAVERY]

I am sending you 2 Paul Forts. Would give you
them but shall want them back in a week or so to write
my article. You must come at Xmas. Ever so many
thanks for long letter : having had a tooth pulled out
to-day can't write much. " Samarkand " has sold 400
copies and it is hoped will sell more.

> Ever yours,
>
> JAMES.

Please send by return *address of Vers et Prose* who
publish *Vivre en Dieu :* it's at bottom of title page.

> *Hotel Stephani,*
> *Montana-sur-Sierre,*
> 10*th Dec.* 1913.

MY DEAR MARSH :

Many thanks for the gleam of hope : but don't be
frightened to tell me if it fades : I am very inured to the
fading of gleams. Many thanks for placing " The Old
Ships " ; will write to Jack Squire and send him another
poem in time. Am trying hard to find a place for
articles in prose, style of Chesterton.

Please be wicked enough to represent *Hassan* as being
rather a better play and more certain of popular success
than *Hamlet* to people interested. It is an odd fact, but
the most important people are enormously impression-
able to the judgment of others.

Has not the Polignac prize been already given to the
Georgian J. Stephens for a work presumably in prose ?
It's prose's turn anyhow, this year.

Do send any hearty friend of yours desirous of
Winter sporting here to Montana (Lunn's run it). It's

one of the best places. I will tell any one who wants to know all about it.

Have finished my novel proofs after 3 weeks' hard work.

Got very furious because *Near East* refused in terror my anti-pro-Turk letter. In despair I sent it to G. K. Chesterton, as Chief Advocate of the free Press and likely to sympathise !

Your kindness is so illimitable that I perhaps dare ask you to lend me a copy of Lawrence's novel, which I will faithfully return.

Ever yours,
JAMES ELROY FLECKER.

P.S.—If you could lend me Gosse's *French Impression* containing Paul Fort, should be immensely obliged.

*Sanatorium Stephani,*
*Montana.*
*10th December* [1913.]

MY VERY DEAR AND ANCIENT FRANKO :

Yes I got the books. And I send you the stamps so long desired. And a little poem I wrote t'other day.

There's just a gleam about *Hassan*. Viola Tree and Alfred Parsons are hugely enthusiastic and want to play it. But of course it will come to nothing.

I don't think, my dear Franko, that I shall be able to go to Lugano or Locarno at Xmas. I shall certainly if still alive and able to move go to Italy in Spring.

Now if you could come there nothing in the world would rejoice my heart more. But I don't want you to curse me. It's a bloody long and expensive journey for you—also the trains *via* the Loetschberg fit bloody badly. Of course if you were an amateur of this sweet Swiss scenery you could crawl here in stages *via* Lucerne, steamer on Brienz lake, Interlaken, Spiez. Otherwise you must come Zurich, Berne, Thun, Loetschberg. Now the sunshine here is very splendid in the snows, and the

Alps are really rather unearthly—but we are really the only attraction for you ! If you hate the cold we might go down to Sierre where there is a most excellent hotel : but really one doesn't feel the cold much in this windless spot. It is rather fascinatingly silly too to roll down hill in a *luge*—a form of exercise that needs the minimum of athletic skill.

But, my dear Frank, I fear it would be dishonourable to lure you here. (I doubt if when you get here you can get a room under 12 francs a day and much your best way would be to get your ticket and all from Lunn's who run this place.) But I can only say that if you did come, you would be most ravishingly welcome. But it's too good to hope for !

Well I meant to send you *The King of Alsander* in proof, but I had no time. I had to rewrite all the end of it again. And it will cost me, as the French say, the eyes of my head for altering the proofs.

It is really rather wonderful in places now !

As you will see from enclosures, have been attempting Blank Verse Virgil. Do you think it's worth while going on—say with *6th Æneid*. It might teach one how to write blankers.

Don't worry about the anthology. I mean I've quite forgotten about most of those Frogs now except Paul Fort, the article on whom is now finished and being copied.

I wrote a *magnificent* anti-pro-Turk letter to the *Near East* to which I had contributed letters and articles before. It was refused. I have sent it to G. K. Chesterton in a fury.

You might like to read this story of Janina by my wife and me in collaboration. Please return.

Ever yours devotedly,<br>JAMES.

" The Old Ships " will appear in *New Statesman*, I hope to write for this paper in future.

*Hotel Stephani,*
*Montana-sur-Sierre.*
16.XII.13.

*To* EDWARD MARSH

Just a line (the post is just going) to thank you for your encouraging long letter. You shall have the scenario by next Monday if not earlier. Of course I leave everything in your hands and Dean's. Please tell the latter that the more detailed his suggestions are the better pleased I shall be, and that I am very amenable. (*e.g.* Suppose even he suggested something I thought was æsthetically wrong, I would content myself with sticking to my version in the published edition of the play.)

My ideas on the Contract I'll let you know by letter. There is, alas, plenty of time for that.

*Please* pay me a visit on your way to or from Rome. Stay a night at Montana. I'm right on the road (Simplon-Milan : stop at *Sierre* and take a funicular up). Will arrange you all things.

Murren is not this way, alas,

With haste,
JAMES ELROY FLECKER.

P.S.—Excellent article on " Samarkand " in December *Englishwoman* (Geraldine Hodgson). Do you know her ? Glad Gosse likes the " Old Ships."

*Hotel Stephani,*
*Montana-sur-Sierre,*
*Switzerland,*
25 *Dec.* [1913.]

MY DEAR MONRO :

Best wishes for Season and *Poetry and Drama*. Please continue my subscription. Last number excellent.

Madeleine Rock very good. Let me praise last verse of your poem! Macnamara and Mr. Frost I cavil at. Goldring has not got his deserts at the hands of the Georgians : he does succeed in something : the others aim high and miss. Tell Flint (if he cares to know) that I am converted to Claudel by " Le Repos du Septième jour." Nevertheless a lot of this rhythmic prose Flint seems to find so novel and inspiring was popularly known in England 20 years ago as Wardour Street.

Now to business. I'm always very pleased to do any reviewing (book post not much dearer than in England) but may I do you a 3 page review of the *Oxford Book of Spanish Verse* just out, if you haven't given it? If they haven't sent a copy I'll get one.

If you would care for some poems let me know. At present I am translating Vergil; *Æneid VI.* into blank verse. What *will* the Futurists say?

Ever yours,<br>JAMES ELROY FLECKER.

*Hotel Stephani,*<br>*Montana-sur-Sierre.*<br>[16.12.13.]

MY DEAR FRANK :

Frightfully sorry you can't come now but would prefer it myself in January. I hear from Marsh that Tree's slumbers are ruined, because he can't tell whether to play *Hassan* or no. Meanwhile everybody's frightfully full of alterations for *Hassan!* Am only worried as to whether the reasons for their not being able to commit suicide during their " day of love " are strong enough. I even thought of an extra scene but the play it seems is too long already. A publisher wants to know if I'll write on the " Future of Poetry." What a bore! By the way I may write to your dramatist (was it Maugham?)

through you one day to know what sort of a contract one ought to get.

Am too flat to write a letter—forgive me.

JAMES.

P.S.—The great thing will be to have you here for a fortnight, later. I do hope you can pull it off. My soul is like a lump of mud, and even the news about *Hassan* merely succeeds in maddening me because I can't be in England. There was a good article on "Samarkand" in the December *Englishwoman* by one Geraldine Hodgson.

[*To* J. C. SQUIRE.]    24 *December*, 1913.

I hope there was nothing in my postcard that suggested that I was disparaging the verse column of the *New Statesman*. All I imply is that with the best contributors in the world one *can't* get one good or even fairly good poem to publish every week.

I told Marsh I had written about this matter to you, the *New Statesman*, and he was, I think a little unreasonably vexed with me. Please don't tell him I mentioned this. I didn't know when I wrote that the matter would come before you at all—and in any case I merely wanted to know whether you could increase the rate for me in future : I wasn't demanding an extra guinea for the actual poem, and if my postcard gave that impression, it was pure carelessness on my part.

May I frankly tell you what has happened to me? The *Nation* has published a good number of poems for me. Its flat rate to everyone for poetry is two guineas. But lately it has taken to rejecting my best work from time to time (including the "Old Ships") and instead of reviewing my last book properly it was given an insolent ten line review with a batch of nincompoops—after I had been working with the paper for years. These insults and snubs are sufficient to make me desire never to write another line for the *Nation* and if the *New*

*Statesman* will treat me better—that is, accept a poem from me as a matter of course once every five weeks or so—the *New Statesman* may be assured it will only get my best work. . . .

You speak kindly of my verse—particularly kindly as I know from your review of " Samarkand " that you are rather disappointed by it. You probably feel—what I feel pretty strongly—that it's one thing not to consider a man a new Browning and quite another to consider his verse good enough for a weekly paper. I take the violently egoistic line that I have never published in my books a single poem which a weekly paper ought not to have jumped at at once. You are by no means bound to take this view !

In any case I send you a poem, and will accept the guinea rate for any further verse I send you, merely hoping that someday you will be able to raise your general flat rate.

P.S.—Did you ever get a letter from me about Diarbekir. Diarbekir is the regular Turkish pronunciation—and all Europeans follow it. Darbekr is Arabic.

*Sanatorium Stephani,*
*Montana s/Sierre.*
*26th* [*December.*]

MY DEAREST FRANKO :

I'm a bit late thanking you for the joyous surprise of Claudel—a twin astonishment for me.

a. I didn't open the parcel thinking it was just some books you were sending back till second thoughts prompted me &c.

b. I had never cared for Claudel in my desultory dippings till I read the first play—the Chinese one—the first act of which is very grand and Dantesque indeed. The 2nd act which I am half way through is a wee bit stiff and tiring.

125

—— to recommence, I'm a bit late in writing to thank you, but as a matter of fact I wrote at once to thank you, but either lost the letter or posted it : I hope I lost it, as it was a rotten letter, because I was beastly weary. I am now in bed with distinct symptoms of alcoholic poisoning due to *Réveillon* festivities, and much more cheerful.

Why I was annoyed at Claudel was this : in *Poetry & Drama* (Quarterly, gave me a bleeding Review but in general very sound periodical which it is your duty and mine to support—will send you this year's 4 numbers if you want them—2/6 a number—10/6 a year Poetry Bookshop, 35 Devonshire St., Theobalds Rd. London W.C.—am I developing a post futurist or bracket style ?)—a man Mr. Flint what does the French, was always puffing Claudel and seemed to think that his Rhythmic Prose was something new and marvellously strange. This cult of " Rhythmic " Prose, anciently known as Wardour St. when you and I were young boys ! tickles the French mind and is a horrid symptom of decay. A Traditionalist like Claudel ought to use verse but he *can't*—his verses are no good. So he uses prose. But if he is going to talk b—— about having in each line just enough for the breath to say, I shall talk b—— too and cut up *Hassan* into versicles and call it poetry.

Do write me a good letter. You never said a word about the 2 poems I sent you with " Janina "—perhaps they missed your eye—perhaps you didn't want to damn a poor invalid.

Do come here soon and help me finish the 6th *Æneid*.

Ever so jolly of you to give me such a delightful present. We both of us send the heartiest wishes for the season and a meeting as swift as the Fates will allow.

Eternally yours,

Js.

# REMINISCENCES 1914-1915

## *ECHO OF A GREEK FOLK-SONG.*

*What token can I send down stream to you in the world below,*
*What little gift of passing things of earth that you loved so,*
*Now that the year is young again and leaves begin to grow?*

*If I send down a pomegranate it sinks and will not float,*
*And if a frail anemone the water spares it not,*
*If a twined branch of budding vine it clings to Charon's boat.*

*Then I will send you down this heart in a kerchief of bright*
  *red,*
*It shall not sink but float bravely, be it in weight as lead,*
*For currents cannot drown a heart or Charon stop it dead.*

*The dark flood straight will carry it and roll it at your feet,*
*And you shall take it in your hand and feel it throb and beat,*
*The red shall speak of life's red rose, the glow of summer heat,*

*The rapid pulse of windy leaves and swaying of the sea,*
*And in the soul spell-bound in peace by the Lethean lea*
*Memories waking, like a swarm of wild song-birds set free,*

*Will shake their new-found sleepy wings with little trills of*
  *fear,*
*Then suddenly maybe a song rising so high and clear*
*Shall bring you back Earth beautiful, fair Spring that was so*
  *dear.*

*H. F.* 1925.

AFTER Leysin we had been to Montreux then to
Montana, then back to Montreux for two months in the
autumn of 1913, returning to Montana in November.
After being very ill during the winter there my husband
wished to change scenery and was once more dreaming

of Italy. We then went to Locarno in March, 1914, and from there early in May to Davos. When the war came on we moved to a flat, the food at the hotel becoming impossible.

Since arriving at Davos he had been either lying in his bed or on a couch and had had some very trying weeks ; but he never spoke of death, though he often worried about the future. The first time he mentioned the end was a morning in November when he woke up and called me. He seemed agitated and said, " I have been dreaming of the New Jerusalem, I was treading the streets all paved in gold and I saw the walls and towers of crystal and amethyst. I suppose I shall die soon."

Then on another November night he woke up before daybreak and sat up writing with a blue drawing pencil on a sheet of drawing paper (at the time I had to prevent him from writing more than about an hour a day for it exhausted him, so he had neither pen nor paper near him but some coloured pencils with which he amused himself, drawing imaginary landscapes. I did not know the end was so near or I should have let him do as he liked and not have vexed him with an interdiction that caused much painful discussion and was cruelly felt by him). When I went near he gave me to read the " True Paradise," and then asked me to write it down clearly there and then.

On Christmas Day he was able to have a nice lunch and eat of a home-made plum pudding, and was in high spirits. On the eve he had asked for the barber and had had a short Van Dyke beard which he wore since Montana shaved off. This altered his looks a great deal, at the same time revealing how much thinner he had grown, so that I could scarcely bear to witness the change that had come over him in a year.

On Friday, New Year's Day, 1915, he seemed fairly restful, but toward 3 p.m. he was seized by a violent fit of coughing which lasted for more than two hours and quite exhausted him. He felt very weak after this, and on Sunday morning, January 3rd, after hearing his heart the doctor told me the end would come in a few hours. In spite of long anxiety this news gave me a terrible shock, for strange to say I had never realised the imminence of the danger. About Christmas, my husband had mentioned he would have liked to take the Communion, so I now asked the doctor to send the clergyman. He objected, saying it might frighten him, but I was certain of the contrary. The chaplain was too ill himself to come but the Rev. W., a patient, arrived about eleven. A tall emaciated figure, he could scarcely stand, but his pale face with the fine forehead and the spiritual flame in the eyes made a great impression. I said to Roy that as it was Sunday and he had wished to take the Communion, Mr. W. had brought it to him. He brightened up and said, " But I can't say my prayers," then I said, " Never mind, the clergyman will say them." He smiled and took the Communion. He thanked the clergyman and said afterwards, " Why did I not meet him before ? " When he had left I said to Roy, " Now you'll soon be better and we'll go to the Italian lakes in a week or so." He answered, " You say that to cheer me up, but . . . I'm quite happy now." And closed his eyes smiling. A moment later he beckoned to a nurse who was standing at the foot of his bed, saying, " Nurse, will you leave us a moment," and looking up at me with a gaze full of light he said some loving words and closing his eyes seemed to rest for a while.

Later he was delirious again. He suddenly sat up and began singing in that musical voice of his but very loudly, a sort of triumphal march in rhythm resembling the Marseillaise. I tried to stop him, fearing it would exhaust him. In a moment he lay back and in a strange whisper without moving his lips I heard him breathe the words, " Lord have pity on my soul," and as I let go for a moment his right wrist which I had been holding tight, he said aloud, " Hold me." Then delirious again he shouted, " Damn, damnation." I said, " Hush, darling, don't say that," and he replied smiling again, " Is it all nonsense ? " " What darling ? " " What I've been saying is it all nonsense ? " And he lay back in perfect calm ; then I heard a little breath and after all was silence. It was shortly after three, the sun was setting behind Davos, through the wide open window one could see the snowy peaks across the valley flushing a bright crimson, and the soul of a poet who had loved the light passed behind the mountains following those " strange voices " that called him yet once more.*

## SOUTH, EAST AND NORTH

O call me call me call me far away
To black Carpathian woods where strange things roam,
And further to the quiet midland sea,
To sunlit meadows of old Sicily,
To white Ægean isles among the foam,
O call me call me call me far away.

O call me, ye strange voices, farther far !
Away to the dreamy painted lands beyond,
Where swing the idle censers whole days long
And all the night is mellow with a song
By women languorously monotoned,
O call me, ye strange voices, farther far.

Call me strange voices, call me yet once more,
Call me to lifeless lands of wind-swept snows,
Where only the myriad eyes of other spheres
Immutably are open. Ah, but there peers
Death in the cold white desert where winds blow,
And those strange voices call me call me yet once more!

*[November 6th, 1904.]*

---

* In one of my husband's copybooks there is an early poem which I give here. It is dated November 6th, 1904, the day after his twentieth birthday; it shows a strange intuition of the lands where his last years were to be spent, and contains the prophetic vision of Death beckoning among the snows.

*Stephani,*
*Montana.*

MY DEAR FRANKO : [7.1.14]

I have wanted to send you some quantitative hexameters which I wrote, having read Stone's essay on
Milton's prosody. I wanted to send you some of my
translation of Virgil. But alas having upset my stomach
on Christmas day, I've been in bed ever since with a
horrible fever which only leaves me for a few hours in
the morning. I have had and shall have for God knows
how long a horrible time, and being not much of a stoic,
am rather despairful. Can't even read much : Do write
to me. Have you read Barrès's *Voyage de Sparte ?*

Ever yours,

JAMES.

*Hotel Stephani,*
*Montana-sur-Sierre.*

MY DEAR FRANK : [17.1.14.]

Let's have a line—quite concerned not to have heard
from you. Am still in bed, alas and alas. My people
came to see me and stayed four days. I asked them to
come—but it rather tired me. Better to-day. They
met in the train at a station called Sion on their way
back that scoundrel Jack Beazley of all people and made
him write to me. He's back from Greece—lucky beast.

Thy ancient,

JAMES.

*Hotel Stephani,*
*Montana-sur-Sierre,*
*Switz.*

MY DEAR MARSH : *Wednesday* [ *Jan.* 1914.]

I have been and am still most evilly ill with fever
every night—ever since Xmas. I can't write anything
and what is worse I sometimes can't read.

At this moment your welcome letter. So, many

thanks for the cheque. I do feel that is most particularly generous of you to treat your anthologized thus ! Compare X—— Y—— of Z—— anthology who tried to get my book free out of me into the bargain !

I send you herewith complete " God Save the King," with your suggestion adopted and a verse added. Do you know Marsh I think it damned good *for what it is*, especially last verse. The *Sphere* have asked me for some poems. I might send it there. But I've half a mind to send it to H.M. (perhaps through Bridges) just for the fun of the thing. There was a magnificently good little article in *Poetry and Drama* on " God Save the King " (it set me off) showing the existing version to be, historically, an insult to the reigning Dynasty. All this is only my fun, not preposterous pushfulness, tell me, O you from whom all good advice flows, whether I shall try on some game with it, or send it mildly to the *Sphere?*

" New Numbers " you have never explained to me, my dear Marsh, but I presume it is a sequel to the " Georgians." Best Luck to it !

And now as for *Hassan*. I will not conceal from you that were I well and not an exile, I should think several times before accepting. I do not believe myself that *Hassan* needs much more alteration than I suggested in the Scenario and which I could make in a week if I were well, and also the Stage-manager's inevitable improvements. I do not believe much in the " stagefying " of dramas : you can't turn *Hassan* into a sort of Darling of the Gods : I don't mean to imply Dean wants to do this. But I am nervous of the mania for alteration theatrical people have. Look at that silly *Kismet*. Tree's " necessary alterations " seemed to Oscar Asche to ruin the play completely. I think you told me this yourself, and lots of B. Shaw's and Shakespeare's most popular plays are hopelessly ridiculous from the construction point of view. But as it is, I accept *unreservedly :* only insisting that he gets to work at once !

To have him financially interested is a splendid guarantee of getting ahead. Please ask him to write at once. I shall accept his alterations as unreservedly as possible, as, after all, I can publish my own text.

I am very cheered by your letter and the Doctor says I'm getting better. I hope to crawl to Lugano in Spring, if I can't get to England, Dean will have to pay me a visit there.

You know I wrote an earlier play, scene in England of to-day, called *Don Juan*. Am longing to be able to revise it. It will make a fine work—because less exotic than *Hassan*.

I think I told you that I had learnt to write really fine blank verse at last by practising on *Æneid VI.* translation. I also sent Monro some quantitative hexameters : I haven't heard from him, he may be rather sorry !

*The King of Alsander* out shortly I hear : but they don't let me know the exact date, I imagine in under a fortnight.

Enthusiasm for me in Boston, whence gentleman writes inviting poems for the Chicago poetry paper, forget its name. Another American has sent the most 'orrible verse translation of Hérédia, which has gone into 5 editions !

The *Fortnightly* rejected "Paul Fort." I haven't written so much since I've been ill. I must end now.

Ever yours,<br>
James Elroy Flecker.

Send my love to Rupert, our Donne redivivus, when you write.

*Hotel Stephani,*<br>
*Montana-sur-Sierre.*<br>
[*Jan.* 1914.]

My Dear Marsh :

As I am feeling a little more alive physically to-day I feel that I would like to follow up my letter of yesterday with a few observations.

My chief point is, please let Dean realize that I shall want to know a bit more of his intentions, and that I shall probably want to bargain a lot, in fact that I want a free hand in negotiation.

I want you to forgive me if anything I say in this letter contradicts yesterday's. The fact is, I'm a bit stronger and able to think things out a bit. I have no doubt that Dean and myself will get along splendidly, but if we don't, please my dear Marsh, don't make a personal point of it. Dean wants a very heavy percentage and he wants to put his name to the play : these are both propositions that I must look into carefully : they are both propositions disadvantageous to me, which ought to be balanced by great advantages. So let it be understood by Dean that you take no responsibility for my attitude ; so that if Dean comes to you and says I'm a bloody bargaining Jew, you won't be cross with me. For above all things I want to avoid offending you in this matter.

I rather wish I could have one last shot at Granville Barker. And if Dean isn't going to get me free I imagine J. Drinkwater, to judge from his enthusiastic letter about a very muddled draft of Acts I and II might accept it without wanting me to hash it all up.

You understand the cleverer Dean is the more exasperating he will be in his alterations. I am very afraid of them. On the other hand, I see an enormously good opportunity of getting *Hassan* played. Please put us in communication as I've said, and a thousand thanks to you for all the pains taken—but please scratch out the words in my yesterday's letter which implied any complete acquiescence in Dean's projects.

I arranged the matter of the *New Statesman* Poems with Squire very amicably, and withdrew all my claims.

Do forgive me for shewing such nervousness about this matter and particularly for having written too hastily yesterday. I hope this may reach you before you've seen Dean.

Ever yours,<br>J. E. FLECKER.

If you have seen Dean already, I would only ask you to modify what you told him with your invariable tact. Tell him I'm nervous.

*Hotel Stephani,*<br>
*Montana-sur-Sierre.*<br>
18 *January.*

MY DEAR MARSH :

I will take your advice and definitely let Dean co-operate as he wishes. Cancel my second letter therefore and say nothing about it. But do remember, my dear man, that when one's writing with a fever of about 102 one's apt to be vague about business principle.

I shall send Godsave to the *Sphere*. Monro's got my hexameters. Immense thanks in any case for having brought *Hassan* to this stage.

I think the line about the Mould of Form is alright : but can't explain it in words. The connection between Space and Form should present no difficulty : form of rhyme (the weft and the woof of alternate rhyming verse) is a good phrase, and surely the connection of time and rhyme—for rhyme is the marking of time, nothing more or less—is right.

Now 'tis quite understood the second letter is cancelled. Let me now thank you for my beautiful Zither which is more lovely than a dream. Why do I thank you ? Because I purchased it with the " Georgian " gold. One can play it in bed. It's hellish difficult to learn— but most interesting, and I can stop reading books— you do not know what a joy that is.

I must return you your books. Do you know I find the *Sons and Lovers* as unreal as a dream. The characters don't seem to hang together a bit. But there, I'm no judge of novels!

I have grown a Vandyke beard. Please excuse the shortness of this letter in reply to your long one; I have to put things shortly: I'm not yet up to much, though, thank the Lord, a good deal better.

> Ever yours,
> JAMES ELROY FLECKER.

P.S.—Once I decide I decide whatever you may think and I shall be an example of cordiality with Dean.

> *Hotel Stephani,*
> *Montana-sur-Sierre,*
> *Switzerland.*
> 31 *January*, 1914.

To J. C. SQUIRE
DEAR SIR:

I enclose two translations—my best work as translation: please choose one (or both): or else return as I shall quite understand if you don't care to publish translations.

Please let me have copy of the *New Statesman* in which my last verses appeared:—I've not seen 'em in print. Wish I could afford *N. S.* every week: perhaps if I become a diligent contributor I shall have it.

Too late to ask to review Chesterton's *Flying Inn?* A magnificent book,—his masterpiece: and the humourous verse splendid.

I am still too ill to do much and quite incapable of writing poetry.

> Yours faithfully,
> JAMES ELROY FLECKER.

*Sanatorium Stephani,*
*Station Climaterique de*
*Montana-sur-Sierre,*
*[Suisse]*
*Feb.* 18—/14.

MY DEAR MARSH:

I'm very sorry not to be able to say that the Spartan Flower * means something specially recondite. It is quite general in meaning, though I hope the phrase is not unsubtle.

I am inclined to think Bridges and Stone wrong about *-ing* which is bold and bad of me. But in any disputed case the obvious *thing is* to mark it doubtful and not worry. Observe that *thing is* in the above sentence is pronounced thing gis !

Monro tells me he first liked, then disliked, then liked the hexameters, and on receipt of " God Save the King," which on second thoughts I sent him, objects to God being brought in and to the Imperialism of it, but will condescend to print it with a note to the effect that it is a highly unsuccessful but interesting attempt (here I am exaggerating his language) and inviting others to try. All this between us—but don't you think, my dear Marsh, that it's all of it damned cheek. My own view is that Monro ought to go on his knees and praise God (whom he is antiquated enough not to believe in) on receipt of any damned old poem I choose to send him, being certain it will be infinitely better than three quarters of the forsaken wash he prints. But far be it from me ever to quarrel with Monro, he is far too useful ! And he has done a great deal for languishing poetry.

I have written a poem and sent it to the *Sphere* who asked for some—rather a Herrick poem : have not heard about it yet.

Dean writes to say he is furiously busy and not very

* Reference to the poem *Oak and Olive.*

well and going to get married, and can't touch *Hassan* till April. All of which ain't very encouraging, but of course it's the best thing.

I am still in bed. I sit up a bit each day. But I'm ghastly sick of it all.

I can't get a line from Goschen, but I see he's advertising the forthcoming appearance of my novel at last.

I have sent a line to the *Oxford Mag.* explaining how I came to figure as a Cambridge poet. The rotten ass (hope not a friend of yours) who edited the Oxford book wants hanging. It strikes me that I don't know whether you are of Oxford or of Cambridge and you seem to lean to Cambridge—but you will let my loyalty assert that I could have edited an Oxford book (on same dates as the Cambridge one) which would have made the Cambridge book pale !

Ever yours,
JAMES ELROY FLECKER.

Of course what I complain of in Monro is not his criticizing, but his having apparently to think for about a month before deciding whether my work is good enough for his speckless journal or after asking for it.

*Hotel Stephani,*
*Montana s/Sierre,*
*Switzerland.*
*Thursday.*

MY DEAR MARSH :

I send you by the same mail the scenario, as well and quickly done as possible, for I am not allowed to work many hours a day.

I suggest that it should be typed (3 copies) at my expense, one copy for Tree, one for Dean, one spare, and MS. returned to me. You will see that the Scenario is of *Hassan* as it stands, but that the alterations which appear to me advisable on this my first rereading since I finished it, are indicated in footnotes. If Tree had better not see the footnotes, have them omitted in his typed copy. Please show these suggestions to Dean.

I do not know how to thank you for the most exceptional pains and trouble you have taken on my behalf. I only hope you will come to Montana to be thanked. I could not come to London even to see *Hassan* played now : but I hope to come in April next, if I'm well enough, and of course to see *Hassan* I'd risk nearly anything.

Ever so many thanks for the books you sent me. Gosse is fascinating : the other one (isn't the title indiscreet ?) I haven't yet read.

I wonder if I might ask you with your wonderful kindness to do me a little but not very troublesome service, only if occasion offers. I have written an essay— pretty careful—on Paul Fort, I sent it to the *Fortnightly*. I was unable to quote Gosse in it because I hadn't read him : I intend to create a reference when I get the proofs : I am gratified to see that Gosse has some remarks in his short study very like my own. Gosse knows all about the essay as I wrote to him about it, but you might mention casually that the *Fortnightly* has it under consideration (Courtney isn't it ?) and that he might like to look at it. Gosse's interest might bring Courtney to accept it and it means a good deal to me, financially. But don't worry, as I think and hope Courtney will accept it in any case.

I can't tell you when *Alsander* will be out : all I know is I am waiting for the final proofs. I presume early in January. . . .

I could not help being rather comforted and cheered by your long letter. At any rate it shows that *Hassan* can be taken as a serious possibility even by the most " popular " managers. But I well know the vacillating character of Tree : did he not vacillate over that entirely silly and paying production *Kismet* ?

By the way, couldn't one make Barker jealous ?

Ever yours very gratefully,

JAMES ELROY FLECKER.

Dean's copy of the Scenario will be very useful for him to pencil his ideas on. Wish I'd got another typed copy of *Hassan*. I have to work from a very untidy MS.

*Sanatorium Stephani,*
*Montana.*
*Tuesday.*
[*recd.* 4.2.14.]

MY DEAR FRANCO :

I'm a bit more alive that I was—but still in bed : thank God with less fever.

I enclose a few brief notes for Freissler.

*Hassan.* I have had to sign a contract with Basil Dean, late head of Liverpool Repertory Theatre. *Hassan* is to be by me arranged for the stage by him. He is to have 25%. I can't help it. He is Tree's adviser and will probably get Tree to play it : he will certainly get it played somehow.

I want to hear what that lazy Freissler is doing : is he getting on with the translation ?

I play the zither like a romantic lady all day. I have grown a Vandyke beard. As for Bourget I never read such boring stuff. He has one supreme shorter, about Iceland, in *Les Voyageurs*, called " Neptunevale." The man has no humour : is 5th rate.

My wife, who knows more than I, thinks " Sinister St. " pretty cheap after the first start off. The incidents lack invention. English realism is drear stuff. Marsh sent me a book he raves about, *Sons and Lovers* by D. H. Lawrence. Coal miners etc. Negatively written—

nothing vulgar. No characters, no passion—a sort of unreal haze of dreariness.

My wife has met your Marcel at Athens years ago.

I will perhaps if you are very good when I've finished reading it for the third time send you Chesterton's *Flying Inn* just out. It is his masterpiece. 'Tis good to hear a great man sometimes, as someone said listening to Barrès's funeral oration over Moréas. Chesterton is great in this farce.

Ever yours,<br>JAMES.

I still hope we may be three on the Riviera next March or April—at or near Portofino. If you haven't seen Max's new vol. of caricature I will lend it you.

*Hotel Stephani,*<br>*Montana-sur-Sierre,*<br>*Switzerland.*

DEAR MONRO : [*early* 1914].

You haven't ackgd receipt of my hexameters from which I infer you weren't pleased. So write and do so. I am not quite so ill now—but weakish and still in bed. I send you a tophole version of " God Save the King," written in answer to excellent article *P & D* March 1913. Please return at once if not wanted. Hope to get short one page review of Spaniards done for you : if it don't arrive by 20th February give it up.

Chesterton's new book is gorgeous besides being dam finely written. How feeble a really great man makes the Georgian splutter seem ! The humourous verse in it is among the best in English ; and I may send you on spec a few lines on it—a review for you to reject.

Write and tell me all about everything. I've grown a Vandyke beard and am learning to play a zither in bed.

Ever yours,<br>JAMES ELROY FLECKER.

*Stephani,*
*Montana.*
*Thursday* [20.2.14.]

DEAR FRANK :

I sent you Chesterton and Paul Fort. No hurry to return.

I send you typed copy of Virgil little proof of a new poem.

Let me have genial criticism and return copy in about fortnight.

I am getting a little stronger very slowly. I sit up a bit, etc. Prevailing idea is Locarno—(Maggiore) as soon as I can get there.

Remember I always live in hope of our spending this spring holiday together.

Do you want to read Conrad's *Chance* and *Old Mole* by Cannan ?

Ever yours,
JAMES.

*Hotel Stephani,*
*Montana,*
*Saturday.* [7.3.14.]

BELIEBTE FRANKO :

In such haste am I for a long and able criticism of that hoary but much renovated *King of Alsander* that I send thee a copy with much love (if you happen to have ordered one beforehand gif it to a friend) hoping for a long and exciting critique (don't worry too much about the psychology—there isn't any). The end of it I wrote here : the iller I am the cheerier I get (last chap but one pretty entire and fairy incident in last chap)— also the Pierrot lump and the recognition scene (with improper joke) are Montanese.

Really truly I am going to be wrapped up and taken to Locarno—the *warmest* place on the lake, in about a fortnight. I progress filthy slow ; but I have no fever to speak of, and I believe if it hadn't been raining sleeting and snowing for 2 weeks I shd. be up.

Thine ever,

JAMES.

P.S.—Englishwomen call a book *exciting*, French *passionant*. O the hid subtleties of this !

Hotel Stephani,
Montana-sur-Sierre,
Monday. [Recd. March 18, 1914.]

MY DEAR FRANKO :

So sorry you are—or I hope have been ill : I should think Mycolisine would do you good. I have achieved a drive ! And we have ordered a large trunk and hope to get to Locarno about the 28th inst.

You're rather ferocious about the poor *K. of A.* but you flatter my vanity by singling out all the pieces I wrote here in Montana quite lately (practically the last 100 pages except the conspiracy chapter) for special commendation. Of course there are rotten bits (especi-ally does the machinery clank when Sferelli is giving instructions about the King to Norman) : but you should not include the 1st 2 chapters in your damnation of the first 100 pages—you are probably like me very bored of re-reading them—but they're damned good. Pages 150–185 you damn with justice.

On the whole I think you expect a bit too much from a very light and fantastic piece of writing. The merit of the book lies undoubtedly in certain definite passages—but in this type of book that is bound to be so. At any rate it seems from the few reviews I've had, to be going to be a popular success—and that is really what I wrote it for. I find there's a real spirit of humorous romance in this book which is pretty novel. It has been compared to Stevenson and (far better) to *The Shaving of Shagpat*. Also you couldn't mistake the style of any ten lines of it on a dark night. It's all hallmarked James.

Gilbert Murray has written me a warm encomium of my Virgil translation which he, like me, considers the best ever made.

As I feel a bit alive again, I've begun seriously revising *Don Juan*. You'll find me in the thick of it at Locarno. The last act wants rewriting absolutely. But I am quite surprised at the excellence of some passages—almost disappointed indeed to find that after three years I can't better them at all.

My collaborator is going to visit me at Locarno about May 13th. Hope you'll be there still and help him in the savage work. He says he wouldn't dream of cutting out the Ghosts—which has reassured me vastly.

Write again soon,

Thine,

Jas.

*Stephani,*
*Montana,*
*Switzerland.*
4.3.14.

Dear Marsh:

This is the hole wherein I lie chained to my kennel. Strongly hope to be packed up and taken to Locarno soon.

My publisher writes: " Your novel will be published on the 10th : please ask your friends to ask for it at the Libraries."

I send you print of a poem which either has appeared or should appear in the *Sphere*.

Ever yours,

J. E. F.

*Hotel Stephani,*
*Montana s/Sierre,*
*Switzerland.*

MY DEAR MONRO :                         22/3/14.

Many thanks for your kind letter. Please say no more !
As for me, I think this revised Anthem of mine is a failure
—the *Daily Mirror*, the only democratic and English
paper existent, whose leader writer is one of the most
talented men of our generation, justly remarks that it
don't bear a crowd lustily howling " O all that dolphined
deep " in chorus. I am thinking of writing a new one
in the metre of my " Saracens."

No, I'm not going to criticise *Poetry and Drama*, or
lose the one advantage of my beastly exile—that of being
unable to make myself offensive to my fellow poets.

I like Ezra Pound as a joke—but good God they take
him seriously. He has given himself a label. Anyone
could write Pound—I'll offer you six pages of indistin-
guishable Ezra at a guinea a page any time you like.

I don't again mind a bit what you and Rupert have
done to poor old God, but if you think your views can
appear modern to a Continental like myself living about
50 years ahead of you in the breathless excitement of the
Catholic reaction, you're mistook.

Poor old Victorians too. I read the Lotuseaters the
other day, and in spite of a few vile lines, it thrilled me
till I nearly wept. Where he gets the Classic touch he
seems to me to soar always—in Lucretius, *e.g.*, the translation from Homer. (You know the last grand lines of
his " Ulysses " almost translate Dante.) And what if
Rupert had written about the milkwhite Peacock and
the Earth and Danae to the stars ?

I'm not a reactionary, but I believe in building on
tradition and in the novelty coming from the inspiration
not as with the futurists from an exterior formlessness
which is damned easy to achieve (I do futurists at from

*Pension Rheingold,*
*8 Via dei Fiori,*
*Locarno,*
*Switzd.*

CARISSIMO FRANKO:
No, No! Don't be so late. Unless you must have
your own doctor one don't rest in Munich when one
can lie in a *chaise longue* at Locarno. Locarno is a
*charming* place: but the brutes at this pension can't
cook: so we can't stay. But as there are 300 hotels at
least, hope to find something real good and if so, shall
have no hesitation in urging you to come and lie up
here on a balcony. It's selfish—because we're a bit
extra lonely here—at Montana we had at least some
friends—but here we don't know a soul. The weather
is perpetual sun—for the last 3 days at least. The Doctor
has ordered me two days in bed—which is rather
boring—to repose from the fatigue of travel. *Alsander*
excellently reviewed in *Spectator* but seen through by a
clever Scot of Aberdeen who declares it to be a *satire*
on the Romantic novel.

Thine ever,
JAMES.

Write again. Come early.

[*To* HAROLD MONRO]

*Pension Rheingold,*
*8 Via dei Fiori,*
*Locarno.*
[Postmark 13.4.14.]

MY DEAR MONRO:
Many thanks for your cheque. Do you perhaps
know any people here whom one could talk to? We
are absolutely alone in a dreary German pension,
whose very inmates we never see, and are slowly

going mad. I wish the deuce we had a Villa at Monti for the summer and I wish you would revisit your ancient haunts. We had a mauve blancmange for lunch today. We suffer.

Thine,

JAMES ELROY FLECKER.

*Pension Rheingold,*
*Locarno.*
[18.4.14.]

MY DEAR FRANK :

Just vaguely remembered I never answered you about German rights of *Alsander*. I shall have to ask my publishers who collar half—but it's sure to be alright. For myself I'm too entirely despondent at present to take any interest in anything whatever—I've been stuck here 15 days in bed except for an hour's drive which upset me. I hope you will be able to wake me up a little. It's a horrid world.

JAMES.

Come soon.

*Rheingold.*

DEAR FRANCO :

Come along as soon as you can. I'm a sorry and pitiable sight : and we both regard you as a sort of Messiah. If you're weary after your journey you shall have a nice *chaise longue* to loll in.

Thine ever,

JAMES.

*Hotel Buol,*
*Davos Platz.*
21 *May*, 1914.

MY DEAR MARSH :

Here I am, always in bed, horribly depressed, unable to write, more on account of sheer despondency than physical incapacity. No more of this! I hold with Butler that a man should be damned ashamed of being ill. Locarno didn't suit me, but it was beautiful to look at, and I had a great friend staying there. Nuisance that I had to leave before Dean could come, so have missed meeting him. I find it hard to take an interest in *Hassan* now, I certainly shan't worry him : in fact I only wish he could do all the work. There appears some chance of its being acted at the Court Theatre, Norwich.

I haven't heard from you for such a long time : do tell me the latest news. I have nothing to do but read all day long—and I feel that if only I could walk the world again I'd never look at another book. G. Moore's *Ave* amused me.

I ought to revise an old play of mine called *Don Juan*, and I want to write a play on Judith.

I suppose you'll be going up the river! A punt and a day up the river in good sunshine, Cher, Cam, or Thames is the best thing there is in England. I almost think the Cam better than the Cher—the latter's a bit too gloomy with trees.

I don't expect Rudyard K. to be in favour of the Government, but he needn't have descended to the level of a potboy.

John Addington Symonds lived some years in this hotel and bequeathed all the rubbish in his library to it.

Do write to me. Where's Rupert?

Ever yours,

JAMES ELROY FLECKER.

*Hotel Buol,*
*Davos Platz.*
*21 May,* 1914.

MY DEAR FRANCO :

A line to thank you for the delightful parcel of books and your letter.

I do hope you didn't have too depressing a time at

Locarno. You don't know how I miss your jolly visits here.

I found George Moore most entertaining. Am beginning life of Walshe. Read also *Tinker's Wedding*.

Have also read *Edwin Drood*. Of course Edwin wasn't murdered but is going to turn up.

Am reading the *Moonstone*—good in a sloppily humorous fashion.

My health is much the same. I find my morals very low indeed and have to read all day so as to keep myself from groaning and moaning. I have just a hope that they'll be able to give me a pneumo-thorax—which is a certain cure. But you must have the other lung alright to stand it, and it's a bit doubtful.

Oh, by the way, you should read the *first* part of *John Inglesant*, at least. But the second part is simply a theological disquisition about the Quietists and others. The author takes no definite Catholic standpoint: indeed seems to wobble towards the English Church considerably.

Rather queer—it appears that in Cromwell's day a little chapel in Paris was the only place in the world where the English Church service was read.

Don't forget to send your " horrid " story to us !

I read in the English paper to-day that a Congregationalist minister writing from Assisi has given up a stipend of £600 a year and is going to preach in the hedgerows.

Ever thine,

JAMES

P.S.—Have finished *Life of Walshe*. I suppose it's pure fiction. It's pretty sentimental in parts, isn't it ? But I enjoyed it.

My wife sends her kind regards. She has found a jabbersome but pleasant Scotchwoman to walk with. I am very glad. It's a devil of a life tending a rather

dismal invalid like me if you have no distractions
whatever.

*Hotel Buol,*
*Davos Platz,*
*Switzerland.*
*Tuesday* [2.6.14.]

My Dear Frank :

Hope you have quite recovered from the flue. Had a
pleasant letter from I. Hodgkinson *re* Goschen. Now
prithee attention. I am revising, considerably shorten-
ing, and vastly improving *Hassan*. Whatever Dean
does to it, afterward, this is *my* version for publication
and the German stage. Will you therefore get Freissler
to send me his copy of the MS. so that I can write in the
alterations. There is very little added so that I hope it
won't give Freissler much extra work. If he holds
passionately to some of the cut portions he can keep
them in. If *e.g.*, he has had the poetry of the ballet
(which I have cut) already translated the ballet can be
kept. He shall have the MS. back in a week : but I
must have it at once, as I'm nearly ready.

Of course one great thing will be that you will be
able to see the corrections. I hope Freissler won't be
very wrath. He must expect to get back his MS. in a
rather lacerated condition.

Ever yours,
James.

*Hotel Buol,*
11*th June.*

Dear Frank :

(Don't have a shock my wife is writing this for me.)

I have your kind letter and MS. of *Hassan*. I don't
mind a bit *Hassan* appearing in its old version in German
and shan't ask Freissler to make any changes. I should
like however to know whether Freissler would be hurt

152

if I collared his beautiful clean manuscript to send to London and sent him my manuscript which is in an awful mess with revisions and re-revisions but quite legible. What I should like most of all would be to stick to his manuscript altogether.

I have cut about 40 pages out of 180 of the play and I think improved it a great deal, at all events for the stage. Don't forget to read Jules Renard, *La Lanterne Noire.*

I don't feel very well to-day so I cannot answer your letter. I shall do so as soon as possible.

Ever yours,
JAMES.

*Hotel Buol,*
*Davos Platz,*
*Switzerland.*
*June?* 1914.

MY DEAR MARSH :

Alas, I'm about as rotten in health as possible. Being of a cowardly disposition I take it badly and of a lively disposition it's a hell. However.

No. *Don't* have the Epilogue, and I would rather not Yasmin, as both are in *Hassan* and I don't want 'em too well known. (But do have anything if you want it— I only give my ideas.) *Please* include " Taoping." What about the all blue butterflies poem? Or " Saadabad "? Or " Brumana "?

Most of the *Poetry and Drama* set of critics spend a lot of time calling me a minor poet because I'm not obscure. But it's true enough, I'm horribly unGeorgian.

I did not like Rupert's new Fish. Give him my love and tell him to write me an important letter.

How I wish someone would come to this hole and comfort me ! Haven't had any intelligent conversation for one-and-a-half years, except a fortnight at Locarno.

Would you be so awfully kind as to lend me *When*

*Bonds are Loosed*, and *Les Copains* (*if you possess them*). I've got very nervous of asking friends to lend me books as they're apt to buy them in order to lend them me, which is sinful.

You know, Dean sent me a MS. of *Hassan* for me to make my own alterations and I with great enthusiasm and skill cut and altered the whole play. Meanwhile Dean wrote and told me he had been working for a week amending the old version. I wrote asking him to wait, as it was no good his working on what was practically a different play. Though he wouldn't confess it, I think he's irritated (rightly) at having wasted a week's work (it wasn't my fault, he never said he was going to begin) and (wrongly) at my having probably made without his help 90% of the beautiful emendations he was going to suggest.

If this sounds as if I was girding at Dean it's because I'm too ill to express myself, I only wanted to say I wish you'd have a look at the emended *Hassan*, it's splendid, it really is. All the slow moving bits cut out, the language brightened, the end of Act IV. immensely improved and precious little lost by the cuts. Dean tells me he has no time to look at it yet as he's rehearsing a play.

Ever yours,
JAMES ELROY FLECKER.

P.S.—Why does no one ever comment on my " Don Juan Declaims " ? Isn't it a very gay and jolly piece ? Or is it not striking ? Impromptu Poem in the style of *Poetry and Drama*—

I'm ill
Bloody ill,
Damned ill
If I were not so ill
I'd get up
And knock the Doctor down.

*Hotel Buol,*
*Davos Platz.*

MY DEAR FRANK :                    *Monday* [22.6.14.]

By now you must have the corrected *Hassan* which I sent before your card with Freissler's appeal. If Freissler is keen he might alter the end of Act IV. in accordance with the new text and add Pervanch's new speeches in the Ghost Scene. The other alterations in IV. and V. are unimportant or else interdependent. His proofs wouldn't be hurt by these.

Of course I'm longing to have a long critique by you on the revision of *Hassan*.

I have made a coat of arms for you thus—if you'd like a lovely coloured copy perhaps my wife will do one— gules and fesse argent with a birchrod vert and 3 Munich beerpots or, a border sable crusilly or.

Ever yours,
JAMES.

*Buol.*

MY DEAR OLD FRANK :                    *Monday* [29.6.14.]

Is it possible that I have forgotten to thank you for Honest John D——* which it is easy to perceive you were villainous enough to purchase in order to lend them to me. After that I am bound to read the stuff and must say it's very hard work. Have had a sore throat lately and vile temperature in consequence—have been in the very lowest depths. Have you read Shaw's preface on Education ? He's a thundering great man, but seems to see Sadists everywhere ! Can't make up my mind whether Francis Thompson is *any* good or *very* good.

Let's hear about *Hassan*.

Ever yours miserably,
JAMES.

* John D—— here refers to two volumes of Dryden's plays.—F. S.

*Hotel Buol,*
*Davos Platz,*
*Switzerland.*
[*July?* 1914.]

MY DEAR MARSH:

Ever so many thanks for the loan of the books. Will send them back soon. Never thought Grant Watson would write so well: it's nicely barely written and he was such an ibsenite gasbag. Of course it rather challenges comparison with Conrad—which makes it seem a little futile.

*Les Copains* is huge fun, must read his poetry—said to be very good. The affection of the Copains is very beautiful. Wonder if the bad man cribbed his last episode (Vercingetorix) from Harry Richmond?

Between us—my unfortunate Father has had heavy money losses—and I've finished with F.O. of course. I may have to look round for a Civil List pension. I imagine there would be *no* chance for me as I'm so young and have done so little except for the fact of my illness which prevents me from even writing for my living; of course *Hassan* may take me out of the " Purée "— but who knows?

I'm just a little better. Do write. Specially about your choice for the *New Georgians*. Let me have the proofs by the way as I've made slight alterations.

Ever yours,

J. E. FLECKER.

P.S.—Give me your opinion about the Civil List.


[Recd. *July* 15, 1914.]

MY DEAR FRANKO:

Ever so many thanks for taking all the trouble to make such a vast list for my benefit.

Are you by now a passionate admirer of Jules Renard?

I've marked a lot of books. I've commenced *Les Copains* by Jules Romains.

Did you notice that *Consolata,* part II had given me the idea of " Taoping."

As for *Hassan* I can't follow your suggestion as my MS. is in London ; it will come back soon I expect.

Ever so many thanks for trying to cheer me up.

*A day later.* Will you, my dear Franco, do me a great favour. I want to get some nonsense as a present for my wife whose birthday is on the 14th instant (it will be too late of course). Wrote to Inquiry Office, Zurich, for address of shops, no answer for a week then to Consulate etc. etc. and then they won't send their damned catalogues.

Dearest Franco, *do* procure me for anything between 10 and 20 marks *anything* you like so long as it is perfectly useless and not a book.

It might be a quaint umbrella handle or something Japanese or a bit of Jap silk for a blouse or a Russian toy or a parasol or anything depicting animals especially tigers or cats or a bracelet or a kimono.

If it bores you dear Frank don't worry. If you happen to see anything do send him by return and I will send you cheque.

Ever yours,

JAMES.

P.S.—Know I am being a bore but would be *very* grateful.

[*July,* 1914.]

MY DEAR MARSH :

So many thanks for your very kind letter. My father can continue to support me, he has written, yet awhile— at all events I can tide over till *Hassan* appears. You see he has lost his capital but still has a largish income. Now if I could apply for a pension, I could legitimately point out that my father cannot afford what he is giving me : but I couldn't apply for (or get) an emergency loan or grant from the Literary Fund which is I presume for people in worse straits. At any rate I do hope *Hassan* will bring in something. Honestly I don't expect to trouble the face of the earth much longer—and as long as *Hassan* comes off I shall expire contentedly.

I thought I said in my last letter that my need was not urgent : sorry if I have given you too much trouble. But I am very glad to know about the Literary Fund as I may be on the rocks any day.

Please let me know about your choice of me for the new Georgians.

I am returning your books to-day.

Please tell Squire that I haven't any poems at all and can't write a line. If he would encourage me I would send him some sprightly articles on the babyishness and prudery of English literature.

*Buol.*
*Sunday.*
[recd. 21.7.14.]

My Dear Frank :

Ever so many thanks for taking so much trouble and for the dolls which arrived safely and are very amusing : Batushka is best with a beard and blue eyes. (Enclose cheque.)

Can't write much as I have a sort of oppression of breathing due I believe to an overfilled stomach. It may also be due to reading the *Daily News.* One wants to walk slowly round England with a large stick hitting all her prominent men on the head with the words Bloody baby go to Paris and get educated.

What babyish stuff English literature is ! Wild boy poets with insane ideas—Keats, Shelley, Swinburne. Shakespeare's great fault is childish stupidity ranting sentimental moralist—Milton the only *man* in our literature outside the 19th century. Look at Dickens. I read *Edwin Drood*. His last work. He was trying to write better and I come upon something like this.

" I will look after the child at all events," said Mr Crisparkle,—interjection by author—" Honest Christian soul ! He meant what he said. Good noble fellow ! " And B. Shaw and Chesterton—just clever children and Marlowe a precocious child. Conrad who writes like a man—is a Pole. Tennyson's *Idylls of King*—Pretty stories for children—and he thought they could be a national epic.

Ever yours very stupidly,<br>JAMES. (Over)

I enclose a cutting *re* Otage. Is it really as good as all that ? Its success too has been surely political.

[27.7.14]

DEAR FRANK :
So sorry to hear you have been worried—but alas am too rotten ill to send you a long letter of consolation, I have your " L'Otage." Do you want it back ? Immense thanks for your vast packet of books—the only thing that keeps me alive. Am horrified at this war business : better not put on a post card my feelings about the bullying of small powers by great. You might send me some day a good book on Catholic Doctrine—but I know I could never come in. I can't narrow my own ideas of morality—and I feel rather sharply that suicide is a justifiable thing. Tell me what diplomatic circles think about the prospect of a general bust up. I am sending you a pamphlet, sent me by Cheeseman, by one Knox of Oxford* (just after your time I think) which

* R. A. Knox.

should console you for much. It is the very best style of Oxford humour.

Ever yours,<br>
JAMES.

" Jammes " is delightful. I wish Belloc did not insult his readers so.

P.S.—Boyishness is not always a fault—I didn't mean I despised Shakespeare. I even read him.

*Hotel Buol,*<br>
*Davos Platz,*<br>
*Switz.*<br>
[*August,* 1914.]

DEAR MAVRO :

Damn Austria. Also damn Austin Harrison. Will you please be so monstrous kind as to rescue my Paul Fort MS. I can't get a *word* out of him.

I am horribly ill—can hardly write. Hope some day to finish ode on Greece. The savage bitterness of its preface would relieve me. I suppose England's going to side with Austria to the kill. *Do* let me have your *Westminster Gazette* letters. Why don't the league protest against the vile Balkan league and Bryce's pompous ineptitudes. Do write me a letter yourself.

All I can do is a few lines of translation of Virgil.

Do write.

Ever yours and very feeble,<br>
JAMES ELROY FLECKER.

*H. Buol,*<br>
*Tuesday.*<br>
[recd. *Aug.* 12/14.]

MY DEAR FRANK :

Yours to hand. Of course it don't matter about *Hassan* there's another corrected copy safe with my

160

collaborator. Am horribly disappointed you didn't
come here : suppose you never got my telegram sug-
gesting it : we're so near the frontier. But I do hope to
see you soon and I am anxiously awaiting a twelve page
letter all about your journey (best felicitations on your
safe escape) and about everything else. You don't
know what a joy it is to be in touch with you again. O
your beloved Germans. They have *exactly* the insolence
of the Bulgarians. It's obvious they want to conquer
and prussianize Europe. I hope you feel horrid against
them. I don't mind their beating the Russians, but if
they crush the French the world will be hell for a long
day.

We live on at the Hotel on tick—that is giving
cheques which can't be cashed. It is an unpleasant
situation : when the few pounds of cash we possess
have gone we shan't be able to buy a thing from the
shops : and any day the Hotel may turn us out. If you
hear of any way of cashing a cheque—any rich fellow
who will send me £12 for a cheque for £12 10/- in gold
do let me know. We meant to take a flat and live
cheaper—but now we daren't. The hotel has cut down
our food to the minimum, and supplies awful horrors.
Yet I am getting just a little better : thank God. I pray
I may at least see the end of this chaos. Do you know
I can really imagine a Swiss or Eyetalian snubbing a
belligerent : *My* country is *not* at war, Sir ; my civilisation
continues as usual : my trains are running to time.

Alas, alas. *Hassan* is stached. And the famous
Embankment scene in *Don Juan* is stached for ever.

I would give something for an English paper ! Such
rumours of naval battles that come to nothing.

Meanwhile I go on reading books and hope for better
things. I confess I shall look to you Franko, to help us
if we get in a fix. My old Mother-in-law is here, poor
old dear, and I'm helpless so my wife has to do everything.

Do write a very long letter as soon as you are less tired.

Your faithful,
JAMES.

*Buol,*
*Monday.*
*Aug.* 14.

MY DEAR FRANCO :

Here's cheque : money always welcome : hope you'll get it in time.  If you wire as you say hour of arrival will send someone from hotel with carriage.  We are only 5 people in hotel—so heaps of room—but you must bargain the price when you get here.

Get out at *Davos Platz* the 2nd station (not Davos Inf).

Will try and shave in your honour.

In haste,
JAMES.

*Hotel Buol,*
*Davos Platz.*
[*Tuesday, 24th Aug.*]

MY DEAR FRANCO :

You don't know with what delight and expectation we await your coming—tempered by fear that the place and the food will exasperate you.  But we hope soon (perhaps you helping in the search) to find a flat.

Managed to get £20 by wire, thank the Lord.

I don't want to write much and we shall have so much to talk about—but do fix a day and let's know !

Come here first—and if it's too rotten or too dear we'll leave.

On 2nd hand information Consul here has no money for cheques—so bring cash.

Ever yours,
JAMES.

162

*Buol.*
*[Sept. 4. 1914]*

MY DEAR FRANKO :

Horribly disappointed for myself—very glad for you (though I hardly think the F.O. would have been such swine as to cut you off without a word after all that discomfort and loss in their service). And I suppose I daren't say " at the end of October then " as I hope you will be fixed up permanently this year. Xmas (if there is to be one this year) at least we'll spend together. Well write me some decent letters as compensation. Next month we shall have a flat and it will be more amusing for you if you come—tho' I fear no room to put you up in it. We have taken the flat for a year—lugubrious prospect ! Would that I were with Shackleton—not to hear the hellish news. There seems no hope for France ! Can one believe in a God that lets Germany triumph—that's the question. For obviously it means hell for the world for hundreds of years. For (as a lunatic bard in the *Daily News*) Russians are at all events sorry for their sins *vide* literature (choking sob goes up from, he said) but Prussians glory to have burnt Louvain. They are infinitely civilized—said Hauptmann replying to Maeterlinck who had called 'em brutes—they have the bible, Goethe and Nietzsche in their pockets. One can imagine the hogs with their cigars (I think of Prussians whom I know somewhat) reading up a bit of *Zarathustra* in the evening to buck them up for a jolly day with bombs on unfortified towns, massacres of women and old men, destruction of an university or so, and despatch of Wolff telegrams. But alas—the beasts are brave and victorious !

Mournfully,

JAMES.

*Maison Baratelli,*
*Davos.*
*(Buol, Thursday)*
*[Sept.* 11.]

MY DEAR FRANK :

Please note new address : we move in on Saturday, so your next letter should be addressed there.

Many thanks for gold safely received : a cheque cashed without horrid loss (wiring costs the devil) means a lot in these troublous times.

But where is your promised letter awaited every day since Sunday : do write. If you don't I shall begin to wonder if we've annoyed you. (I always do when people don't write.)

If you *ever* come to Davos we can put you up at the flat just for 5 francs a day or so (this hideous lack of generosity being due to the fact that I have no money of my own in the world) for as long as you like as we have a spare bedroom in which thinking of you we had specially inserted a bed.

I have acquired a regrettably wide acquaintance with the late Victorian novelists. I mark 'em thus :

## Class I

Maria Edgeworth (Of course not in period but aren't the *Absentee* excellent.)
F. Annie Steel. *On the Face of the Waters* (wonderful tale of Indian Mutiny)—rather stiff reading—exquisitely just minded—you must know it. Is she before Kipling ?

## Class II

Mary Coleridge. *King with Two Faces.*
(Vasa of Sweden : rather weird & wild. *Fiery Dawn* by same woman, damn boring.)

164

*A Lake of Wine*. Bernard Capes. Praised by Henley. Damned exciting.

*Troy Town* by Q. (I give *Dead Man's Rock* but I think I give too the Scilly Island book—I forget its name.)

*J. Or Hobbes*. (Some silly rot about a Prince—amusing.)

Hichens *Londoners :* (I roared).

## No Class

Hichens *Garden of Allah, Bella Donna*.

Sarah Grand. *Heavenly Twins*. (Twins good. As for the rest I think the story is to prove that a man who has a woman not his wife before marriage is unfit to marry because his baby will turn out siph-struck.)

Come Franco, tell us all about it and the new Pope, and the temper of the Minister which from the announcements he sends to the papers etc. seems short. I suppose he is annoyed at those bloody polytechnics who got home by themselves, with fool's luck and then wrote to the papers (I have the par.) saying the Minister was keeping tourists from returning quite without reason. My sympathies are for H.M.M. and his staff.

Thine ever,<br>JAMES.

*Maison Baratelli,*<br>
*Davos Platz.*<br>
*[Sep.* 17.]

[*To* MR. FRANK SAVERY]

Your wire and card to hand O *caro* Frank—heartiest congratulations from us both on the merited advancement—are you likely to become V.C. at Berne ?

*Don't* say you didn't get my letter pointing out *change of address*. We are now in new flat with pine panelled sitting room. Don't want the great letter (which I hope will not be long being coughed up) to stray.

Get a week's leave (local) to come and see me as soon as decent.

Have invented a system of writing my opinion of books and things in scraps of paper and putting 'em in bag.

I scrapped *Jane Eyre*—surely the worst book that ever appeared. Classic! What tosh. I admired *Villette*.

JAMES.

Again heartiest congratulations from us both.

*Maison Baratelli,*
*Davos Platz.*
*Sunday* [*Sept.* 21/14.]

MY DEAR FRANCO:

I cannot answer the great letter (which arrived instanter with telegram) just now. The flesh is very weak—and the spirit—just exercised in much bad war verse and in article for the *Westminster*—a little exhausted.

I never detailed to you my feelings when stopped by a hideous Arab crowd with rifles and mad with panic. I only know I kept my head and spoke very good Turkish. Also I had driven to the Consulate knowing that 7 Europeans had already been killed in the streets, and sore at heart that Cumberbatch hadn't sent a *cavass* for me and wouldn't want me when I got there. Indeed I found the place empty and unguarded and the old boy upstairs taking photos—and was sent away at once to look after my wife despite my protestations—and in the back journey nearly got killed as I told you. Well I can do my duty and I can keep my head but I'm a dirty coward—nervous as a dog. If I have to go to the dentist I'm a wreck for days before (until I'm used to it and go every day) and I was bad for days after the event at Beirut. Unlike you I should have sighed with huge joy at crossing the Swiss frontier.

All the same as a soldier with comrades I should do fairly well. At Agde where the mob wanted to hang me and Knox on the *Lanterne*, I enjoyed myself hugely. But O this nervousness of the devil!

I'm damned sorry you've been turned out of the country of adoption. Perhaps you will return some day. I know very well there is something decent about the Bavarian nature which does not exist in the French. The French are never friends.

Meanwhile—take care of yourself.

*Take a leave* as soon as work simmers to ordinary, even if you can't come here, take it: or you'll bust up and be no use to anyone. I strongly advise you to come here for a few days in the beginning of October when the weather is usually excellent (snow to-day everywhere!) If the altitude worries you you'll have to trot a bit lower: I don't think it will. No one (*e.g.* my aged ma-in-law) seems to mind the change after the first day and it's healthy.

Ever thine feebly,

JAMES.

P.S.—You ought to have better arrangements about burning those cyphers. If the Police had come in and refrained you politely from burning 'em after the Declaration of War, would they not have been within strict international law?

*Davos Platz.*
*Sep.* 29, 1914.

[*To* MR. FRANK SAVERY]
MY DEAR ANCIENT:

You are wicked enough not to write no more. But you are cross because I wrote so insufficiently in reply to the Great Screed. Alas, the flesh is insufficient these days and I'd rather talk about it. I know a point occurred to me since—you thought you were in peril from the officials. Why? Surely you were in none but only from the mob. The police might have stuck [? you] in a fortress but nothing worse.

All the same defend your Bavarians, sir,—does Austria behave like that (your tale is not unique)—or France. (It's true someone hit the Kaiser's Consul at Marseilles in the eye with a bottle)—but that was an *apache*. Does England behave like that?

And tell me how far you think all the Awful Stories are true or excusable. Thank heavens, the Balkans are quite out of it.

I on the other hand am doing my duty by writing a pome in which the Germans are *not* called

> shamble breathing sharks
> bloodsteeped assassins
> spike booted baby tramplers
> sons of Hell and Death.

Nevertheless I call 'em some names—for pedantry. What bloody hypocrisy our sudden love for Belgium was—to mantle the fact that we had a moral obligation to France.

Those who have time or inclination to read all French books, many English, some German, apply to Librarie Richard, 80 rue du Rhône Genève.

If it would comfort you to have your books returned, please say so.

My wife sends greetings—only do write to an unhappy devil if you can't appear in person.

Thine,

JAMES.

I can't end up my consular envelopes so I shoot 'em on you. If you aren't an hofficial, send 'em to an hofficial at least.

*Maison Baratelli,*
*Davos Platz,*
*Switzerland.*

MY DEAR MARSH :          *2nd October.*

I know you're horribly busy. I also feel sure your kindness will excuse my impertinence. I can at least go straight to the point.

Enclosed please find a War Poem. I believe an excellent one, as such things go. I was going to send it to the *Sphere*, the only journal which I know will take it, when I thought I would like it to appear in some better place—*Fortnightly Review, Daily Chronicle,* or best of all *Times.*   Therefore :

(1) Could you enclose it with a word to the Literary Editor of *The Times* who reviewed " Samarkand " as well at your suggestion ?

(2) Or send it anywhere else you think would be better than the *Sphere*.

(3) Or send it in enclosed envelope to the *Sphere* if there's nothing better to be done.

(4) Will not worry you by any consideration of the price to be paid for poem. But as *Sphere* offers £3. 3. o it's no good sending it to *New Statesman*, for instance.

Now if you're too busy, or think the poem rotten please pack it off in the enclosed envelope to the *Sphere* at once.   It's only my vile ambition !

I've written this in short fits : it has cost me a lot physically—almost as much as looking over which at the beginning of my illness I sweated out fevers.

It's better to be in one's own flat. But I don't make progress enough even here. However, I'm much better than in July.

Yours timidly,
JAMES ELROY FLECKER.

*Maison Baratelli,*
*Davos Platz,*
*Switzerland.*
*October 6th.*

MY DEAR MARSH:

Such is the pestiferous perversity of poets they are ever scratching at their work, but I am bound to send the new version of these 12 lines to be pinned onto the MS. because I have just found the old don't make sense, and the metaphors were badly mixed.

My free permission if anything—a line here or phrase there in the text worries you to cut it out.

If you are still working like hell I am direfully unfortunate! But I was encouraged because you found time to write to me.

Ever yours,
J. E. FLECKER.

I tear off the other half to write the lines on.

We fight the hardest men their State could forge,
An army wrenched and hammered like a blade
Wrought in Damascus for the Caliph's son,
Dipped in that ice the Pedantry of Power
And toughened with wry gospels of dismay.
Such are these who brake down the door of France,
Brave wolves, braving the horror of the world
Hunting Peace not to prison but to Death,
But even as some brown songbird whose soft nest
Gapes robbery, darts on the hawk like fire
So hath Peace answered, angry and in arms,
And now etc., etc.

Emended lines for the Burial in England.

J. E. FLECKER.

*Davos.*

My Dear Franco :                   *October 8th,* 1914.

Come along now : you don't mean to say you have to
work on Sunday, do you ? Because you are under no
obligation whatever to work longer than from 10 to 6
*qua* Consular official (see Year Book). And as I refuse
to believe you are saving the Empire from Berne I
insist you should take a few days holiday on the hills
near Berne. . . .

I send herewith item 1 war poem in my green book
which please return at leisure. It's very good according
to my wife. But I insist you should read the " Old
Ships " again—if you don't like it—there is no salvation
in you.

I have scratched some recollections of the East lately
and revised Paul Fort to make him up to date by pre-
tending he had a lot to do with the present war. The
" Ode to Greece " grows and grows and never ends
and I've got some pretty poems on England too. But
oh how little I can do a day.

Charles Peguy, *Mystère de la Charité de Jeanne d'Arc.*
Know you this astounding mystic work deformed by
hideous echolalia ? After your heart, Franco. He's
just dead in battle.

Artzybachef *L'extrème limite.* The most appallingly
miserable book (three death beds) I ever read. After
your heart, Franco.

The Countess of Cardigan's memoirs is the dirtiest
book in the English language. Bad, with one good
funny and one good grisly tale.

If you want to bust with laughter read anything by
de Flers and Caillavet.

You send us here from your shop dirty little bits of
paper with very stale news. It is whispered that the
F.O. now gets all its news from the *Corriere della Sera*
and wires it to Berne.

Anxiously await letter about what the *Daily Mirror* calls (everyday twenty times for two months) the German Huns and my pome.

Badly want to see copy of English paper with your question in Commons. Who asked it? How was it answered?

Thine ever,<br>JAMES.

[*To* MR. F. SAVERY]

*Davos*.<br>[*Received November 1st*, 1914.]

So sorry old man : my sympathies now and ever. Don't write till you feel inclined. Horrible pleurisy last night : wife up all night with me : nearly died of pain—and then of anti-pain drugs. Better to-day. Send only poem and B. Shaw when read at once. Will write a poet *versus* B. Shaw. He's so sensible and goes so mad. But about Grey more autocrat than Kaiser quite all right and the Belgian fable.

JAMES.

*Maison Baratelli,*<br>*Davos Platz.*<br>18*th.*

DEAR MR. SQUIRE :

(1) Infinite thanks for speaking to Chesterton about Italian article. Try anywhere you think of. *New Age : Westminster Gazette :* Please have two shots for me ; then return. If postage counts up, send acct.

Couldn't I do up the purely Futurist bit for you as a literary article and leave out the politics (except as illustration). There's good literary stuff in that part.

(2) Have sent purely literary and amusing article (Philanthropists) to *New Witness*. Write to-day to tell them to hand it to you if they're full. I sent it them because you had Italy ; it's just the thing for you.

(3) Thanks for accepting poem and for guinea and

information *re* Marsh. Horrors, he must be wrath with me worrying him to hawk my verses.

(4) If you in your turn get " Philanthropists " and don't want it, do do me the *infinite* kindness of sending it (a) to *Westminster* (b) to *New Age* or (c) back to me if that fails. You don't know what a help it would be to me tho' I know it's a bore to you. Am a bit better.

Yours faithfully,
JAMES ELROY FLECKER.

[*To* J. C. SQUIRE] 1914.
Let me know by return if you like the idea of a jolly bang at the Cambridge Local examination (timed for the sitting Dec. 10–20) with a whack in it at B. Shaw (what a *grand* article of his on the War, I've had the luck to hook with my copy of the paper) and at Educational Reformers generally. I approve of exams, schools, masters, detention and punishment—but I want 'em good. Is there anyone else that sees that education only wants a little joy of life ?

Ever yours,
J. E. FLECKER.

Wish you could send me *New Statesman* regularly. If my Father (Headmaster) gets on my urging 50 copies of B. Shaw on loan for the boys I shall *claim* it. It's much better than it began.

[*To* J. C. SQUIRE]
*Maison Baratelli,*
*Davos Platz.*
*Nov.* 1, 1914.
Many thanks for publishing " Forgotten Warfare." Your letter and paper received alright.

Do if you can, publish this very carefully written article on Italy at once. I shall be very troubled if you cannot—I have taken such pains with it. I am such an enthusiast (and somewhat of an authority) for Balkan

Politics. Also the first part is I hope really amusing and enlightening. It is not I know the *New Statesman* that will refuse to publish it for the sake of not displeasing anybody and the Vallona business is intensely topical.

If you cannot please be good enough to send it on with a word of explanation to the *New Witness*, 21 Essex Street, W.C.

I also send a little poem for you, topical indeed, but of the Season not of the War. I have exhausted myself writing heroic great war poems and intend to write several like this. I will send you more if you like them.

I thought of translating Déroulède's great poem on what a splendid peace we shall have when War's over— but it's 48 lines long and I could only do it on a 3 guinea commission. A most striking thing though for the present moment ! If you care to offer.

Please

(1) In your next p.c. let me know how much you sent to my bank for " Forgotten Warfare " and I will be sending, I hope, for " Italian Attitude "—a detail always of interest.

(2) Let me know if you've seen Marsh lately. I wrote so sumptuous a war poem that I had the indiscretion (tho' knowing he was frightfully busy) of sending it to him to send to the *Times*, and have not heard since.

I am very ill unfortunately and unable to write much— I ought to have kept off this Italian article which exhausted me horribly, so do not fear that I shall plague you further for a long time.

> *Maison Baratelli,*
> *Davos Platz.*

MY DEAR MARSH : 18*th Novr*.

*Beastly* sorry to have bothered you with Poetry. I hear you work from 8 a.m. to 2 a.m.

Don't answer this. I shall consider myself free to

hawk the poem from December 1st on my own account.

If you have been quixotic enough to start any negotiations a postcard or (perhaps less trouble for you) a wire (cut this out for the slave)

Flecker Baratelli Davos Platz,
Stop.

will effectually prevent my spoiling your kindness by messing in on my own account.

Sincerely apologetic—but remember you wrote to me—and though you said you had 12 hrs a day you didn't suggest 20.

Ever yours,
JAMES ELROY FLECKER.

You ought to be practised enough by now not to divest your characters of every shadow of individuality they could possibly have by making them express your own idea of them with infantine exaggerations. And the idea is rather foolishly *Milleyesque*. Après tout, M. with all his intellect cannot read Swinburne : the fault is M.'s not Swinburne's. Nor does a romantic affection for Latinity stamp a man with the seal of enlightenment. And I am rather tired of hearing the Pompous stupidity of Dr Johnson praised by the modern school. Nor is Suckling a poet of very great importance, not to be compared for an instant either as poet or as man with Shelley. Common sense is only vulgar sense : a true sense of the proportion of the world would drive a man nearly mad. Read my dear child * the poem I have just written : I fear no comparison with Suckling.

Ever yours dully,

JAMES.

### III

*Dean Close School,*
*Cheltenham. Monday.*
[Postmark of despatch, November 5, 1907.]

MY DEAR FRANCO :

Your letter arrived—so long expected—while I was writing furiously in a state of such divine inspiration as I have not known for many a long day. It was a wondrous essay on Pentheus making him the type of all Philistinism. Inspired by a careful reading of the " Bacchæ " which has thrilled me more than anything I have read since I first opened Swinburne. . . . Tomorrow in the grey and misty morning, with a corresponding light of reason, I shall revise the sheets which

---

* The poem enclosed in the letter is an early draft of *To a Poet a Thousand Years Hence :* it bears little resemblance to the final version.—F. S.

are written so fast as to be almost illegible, ten pages in an hour and three quarters—and I shall find that the work, like most of such inspirations, is a piece of slovenly poetical prose with a good idea here and there. Then I shall send it to the *Academy*. Do you read that surprising paper? Last week had criticisms of poets by me, unsigned, and the " Dirge," which I sent them years ago before it came out in the *Bridge*, signed. Next week will contain a long letter by me defending myself from the attacks of their own critic of which I enclose a copy, please return. The number after that should contain " Pentheus." Next month's *Albany* will, I hope, contain a long article on the spirit of mod. poetry as exemplified in the " Shropshire Lad," pedetentim progrediamur sounds like Lucretius.

I sent copies of the *Bridge of Fire* to Raleigh, John Davidson and Arthur Symons. Enthusiastic letters from all. R. liked Rioupéroux, Mary M, and the Ballad of the Student, in wh. he caused me to alter one line. John D. was wildly enthusiastic about nothing in particular : most notable book by young man he had ever seen etc : Arthur Symons said that Dolly poem haunted him. Wish these beggars would print their opinions in *The Times* or the *Daily Mail*.

Damned exam : unannounced. When shall I see you again? Bills enormous : hope for the best, *e.g.* Limerick ; Home affairs smooth at present.

Wrote French translation of my lovely new and enlarged version of the Last Generation. It's going to Pimodan to be hustled into a French paper. Star of my Euripean Rep.

My dear Franco, I must confess. Little enough that I shall ever write will appeal to you. The beggar in the *Acad.* is really right ; I do like Pierrot and his moon. And whatever I take up from Tariff Reform to Carpentering, it is merely a huge jest to me, a little Dionysiac dance of my pen through statistics and such follies, just to show that I can do it, And as for the simple poetic style I use it to be surprisingly and powerfully brief, just as I used the old style to be amazingly preposterous.

The novel goeth slowly. It is all sketched out. I hate the details so. I am at sea the minute I get out of my poetry or my satire.

There is a poem " Ideal " in the *B. of F.* which I think you ought to notice. I think it is nearly the best.

The dedication I know appears superficially weak, But I think it is saved by its feeling and simplicity—and may pass for what it is—a dedication.

True, I believe, the *Monthly Review* has, so to speak, croaked. My last Meredithian effort on Laurence Hope must have stuck in its gizzard.

As soon as you have seen this week's and more especially next week's *Academy* write again your opinion of

Your ancient,

JAMES.

Excuse total madness of this letter due to a wineless revel over Dionyse.

[Scribbled on the envelope are the words :—" Can't find *Academy* cutting. Perhaps you read it."]


## IV

*D.C.M.S.,* i.e., *Dean Close School,*

*Friday.*

[No date, probably written in last days of 1907.—F.S.]

DEAR FRANCO :

   a. What in H—— are you doing ?

   b. Am still prisoned here, and sulky.

   c. Read me on " Fiona Macleod " in to-day's *Academy* and tell me what you thought on it.

d. I think the *Witch of Edmonton* is a very fine play, though rather wildly constructed. What say you? The Virgin Martyr appeals to me less : pretty in places. Have just finished a splendid Spanish novel; wish you could read it. You ought to read a translation (said to be bad) of one of Emilia Pardo Bazan's books, published by Lane, and tell me what you think of it. I haven't read it.

e. Novel very near close and no news from Grant Richards. Joyous New Year to you. Xt, I am weary of life.

(There is no signature.)

V

10 Jesus Lane,<br>Cambridge.<br>[Undated.]

[This letter was obviously written after Roy passed his first consular exam : and went into residence at Cambridge : I suppose it must date from some time in 1908.—F.S.]

MY DEAR FRANK :

In sooth a varied prospect. To sit in my most comfortable and pretty rooms discoursing to Charles Raven who sits next to me at the B.A. table at Caius —where they treat me handsomely. Well, life is multi-coloured.

The nov. is under course of typing : at enormous expense I am having a second copy made to send to you. It will come in detachments, of about 4 chapters at a time.

I think I shall be fairly happy here. It is a parody of Oxford, but at least one is earning money. And that makes a vast difference.

I am still reading that glorious book *Tom Jones*.

I will write to you specially about the novel when I send the first detachment.

Is it quite impossible for you to spend a brace of days with me ?

Yours rather sleepily,

JAMES.

## VI

*D.C.M.S.*, i.e., *Dean Close School,*

*Tuesday eve.*

[Undated, but postmarked at Cambridge, April 21, 1908.—F.S.]

DEAR FRANKO :

Was it possible ? Pictures and books to pack, letters to write and the Foreign Office to keep into communication with. No word from Peckham, but do write and say if you can manage the Cambridge Plan : the completed novel only awaits your critical eye and ear.

In haste,

JAMES.

[Peckham is W. D. Peckham, who was a friend of ours at Oxford : he was up at Corpus, and was of the same year as we were. He passed into the Levant Consular Service a year before Roy, and it was really his example which gave Roy the idea of trying for that service.—F. S.]

## VII

*The Union Society,*

*Cambridge.*

[Undated, but postmarked at Cambridge, May 1st, 1908.]

DEAR FRANKO :

Sorry you can't come here. You cld. take a return from Brum or somewhere and so use the whole of your

Manchester ticket but it wd. be v. expensive. Alas Franko, I doubt if you will ever see the novel till it gets into print. The xpence of duplicating even a little of it shewed me I can't afford it. It would have meant a bill of about 8 guis for typing alone. As it is it will cost me about a fiver.

Besides I can revise no more. I am weary.

It is possible that my story starts in tomorrow's *New Age*, if not in next week's.

JAMES.

## VIII

10 *Jesus Lane,*
*Cambridge.*

[Undated and envelope not preserved, probably written in September or October, 1908.—S. S.]

MY DEAR FRANK:

I got your letter at Bologna and am awfully glad you have had the luck to get away from Limbo for a time. When *am* I going to see you going. You may stay with me any time during term.

Had far too good a time in Italy with Toto. Much too good. Sulky at being back here with finances in ruin. Sulky at being unable to write anything at all. Nothing, blank nothing for 3 months. We saw *all* the pictures in Italy. If you are back in England, come and week-end here at once. One has not too many friends *dans ce monde-ci*.

As we stayed in nearly 40 towns in the north of Italy I can't detail you my tour; you must come here.

At all events write X wanst,

to
JAMES.

## IX

*Dean Close School,*
*Cheltenham.*

[Undated, but postmarked in Cheltenham on September 30, 1909.—F. S.]

MY DEAREST FRANK :

It is very irritating of you to be so perpetually absent in foreign parts. For I do long to see you again. I have written a book on education which I can't get published just yet, and sundry poems and tale in the eastern style which is a beauty. I have done nothing exciting this vac except getting myself engaged to a certain Miss X—— whom I met at the Fabian Camp, to the wild delight of my people and complete satisfaction of myself. We shall not marry unless we find we are still suited to each other in the spring. I think it will be a success. She is eighteen months younger than I, very pale face and blue eyes. As a matter of fact I am damned fond of her ; she will make a damned good comrade, is an enthusiast for my writing and never disturbs my work.

Ever yours,

JAMES.

## X

*42 Rue Perronet,*
*Neuilly, Paris.*

[Undated, but postmark in Neuilly on March 23, 1910.]

MY DEAREST FRANKO :

Be damned to you why did you not write, and say you were in England ? Shall be back in 4 weeks, and will simply have to see you.

Seems I'm not going to have any reviews of my new book of poems. O Franko be a sport and earn money

for yourself and fame for me by a goodly article—yea
and fame for yourself too.  I *will* not be in a hole all my
life.

It was Freeman who told me you were at Silverton,
near Exeter.   Am in a very dull hole working.

I sent you a notice of the book did I not,

Pub. Adelphi Press,
11 Adam Street, Adelphi.
Thirty-six Poems by
James E. Flecker,

*5/-*

Eternally thy,

JAMES.

XI

42 *Rue Perronet,*
*Neuilly, Paris.*

[Undated, but postmarked in England on April 4, 1910.]

MY VERY DEAR OLD FRANK :

A joy to see you again, even through an inky mist.
Yea, write the article, O Frank ; beware—owing to
carelessness of publishers who never sent me a revised
proof :

1.  " Arnaldos " is a translation from the Spanish.

2.  " Mignon " from the German.

My dearest Franko, you adopt perilous paths of
criticism in which no one can tread better than yourself.
Jack, who saw them all and dislikes " Western Voyage "
most of " The Town without a Market,"—as it appeared
in the *Nation* it had a lot of literary phrases which I have
struck out—Jack is a meticulous critic : you want the
spirit of the thing.

Points for your article :

1.  Same old unmodest James.  If you think that I
rank with Yeats, Housman, Kipling though a little
below them, and am on a different level to their filthy

N. W. T. H., I pray you say so. It is only saying that I write poetry after all.

b. Criticise the masques as poetry if you like. But they are not void of the true spirit of me which is a hugeous humour. Masque I. was sung in Canterbury Cathedral: when I imagine some good voiced pork-chopper singing about

> My children who are *very* wise
> stand by a tree with shutten eyes
> and *seem* to meditate *or* pray

I rejoice in my heart, Surely it is a jolly well-written verse exercise. And those splendid asses trailing along their robes in the snow. O for a picture by Aubrey! I think it is a vivid scene for so wee a drama. No, Franko, it's the one uniting thing that binds my work together, this humour—even the hugeous nonsense of the shadowgraph humour combined with what the gentleman who in the *Gloucester Echo* wrote about the Unconventional Poems of a Clergyman's son calls my "yearning sadness." In my old style poems—the tourniquets, cinnabar, portcullis, and all the rest of it of Bathrolaire just delight in welding the so absurd words and the sentimental humour of

> men with other Maisies

all one piece—but this sentimental humour to be clearly expressed—in the Roman way,

Enough O Franko. What think you of the Saracens? The East influenceth: read this I send you and *return* it—for I have written emendations on it—will send you another copy afterwards Enough of my pig self, must write a rather complete ballad of Iskander Rumi in 50 verses or else betake myself to the tongue of the Turks. O Franko, write me that article. Have appealed to Maurice for a review.

Thy,

JAMES.

Flourish O Frank, and make a lot of money and matriculate that pup.

Why not keep a restaurant at Cambridge ?

["Maurice" is M. H. Woods, who was at Trinity with Roy but a year senior to him : at the time this letter was written he was by way of being in politics.]


## XII

42 *Rue Perronet,*
*Neuilly, Paris.*

[Undated, has been preserved in the same envelope as XI. I think it was probably written a week or two later. I remember writing the article on his poems for which Roy had asked, and, to judge by this letter, I must have sent it to him in Paris.—F. S.]

My Own Dearest Franko :

Yours to hand. Alas, Franko it is a lone, lone world, and my love affairs are very bumpy : and the thought of still having some friends is most dear to me. God knows if I shall ever marry. If I am all lone lone in Türkei come and see me O Frank.

Says the *Morning Post* 31 March.

" Satiety, wantonness, fear of old age and death are characteristic of the joy of life in Mr Flecker's page. For not only do we feel sure that they are valiant affectations, but there is practical evidence in the beauty of some of his rhythms, images and combinations of words that he has adopted them out of fidelity to his time rather than to himself. The fantastic sonnets of Bathrolaire are full of joy, notwithstanding the words describing horror and shame and sickliness. The humour of the ' Ballad of Hampstead Heath ' is only possible to healthy high spirits."

Then it quotes Mr Judd. Not bad for a reviewer : of, course I am inevitably blamed for "wantonness" etc., and the review on the whole is not very encouraging, but it is better than most.

Now Franko,

a. If you're going to get the article into a review it must be at least half as long again.

b. Leave out the non-Christian part of it. This is not cowardice—but why worry—it don't come out in my verse particularly and is rather unimportant. Nobody is a Christian now-a-days who could possibly want to read poetry.

c. Emphasize the humour.

d. Emphasize the fact that *healthiness* as opposed to decadence consists not in subject but in treatment and technique.

a. in the directness clearness and shapeliness of the images,

b. in the strength of the versification.

e. I think I ought to be a popular poet. For why? My poems, even if failures are interesting, I think, because the subjects are varied and not badly chosen and the treatment definite.

Yes, I think the beginning of your article v. good but the rest is rather disconnected for a stylist like you. It must be the Dalmatian ague from which I trust that you have by now completely recovered. I am drowning love-pangs in work. God be with you. Return the tale when you send the new MS.

JAMES.

## XIII

*42 rue Perronet,*

*Neuilly.*

[Undated; envelope postmarked in England on April 8, 1910.]

MY DEAR OLD FRANKO:

Gad, you're a genius, and were it not for the shameless way in which you have belauded me, I should call you a great critic. Take no notice whatever of my pencillings, beyond what you think fit ; have it typed (see ads in *Academy*) at sixpence 1000, and send to *Fortnightly*. (For addresses see Writers' Year Book, 1/-) If they refuse send to A. P. Watt, mentioning me (their address is in Writers' Year Book too) : if Watts won't take it try,

> Professor Walter Raleigh,
> Hincksey,
> Oxford.

Really I do think it's extraordinarily good as a piece of English.

I must no more now : must work grimly. Tomorrow shall visit E. and F.—woman just arrived—Madame, I hear, much better.

Read the article with the titles of my three books (if you include " Last Generation." *New Age* Press) and publishers of my books and dates.

'Tis definitely off with my Lady at last, for next year or so.

> Thine,
>
> JAS.

If you only *knew* how you buck me up. You make me almost hearty like Mike Furse.

[" Mike Furse " was a don at Trinity—of the manly Christian type, so far as I remember.—F. S.]


## XIV

> 10 *Jesus Lane*,
> *Cambridge*. 7. 1910.

HEIGH FRANKO :
Sad. If you send it to Raleigh (whose address is Ferry Hincksey, Oxford) don't mention that it is my suggestion you should do so, but just ask him if he could suggest an editor. You might write him a pre-

liminary letter asking him if it's any good your sending the MS. He's *very* slack at replying.

Am bracketed 1st in my exam. As I was fourth in the intermediary with a bad second class, it is good to be 1st class and 1st. Such a long time since I floored an exam.

Up to town morgen. See my girl who wired for me to-day. Why? 'Tis an odd world. Come here next Friday?

Thine,

JAMES.